THE BOCAS

and

THE BULLDOG

The story of sea communication
between Trinidad and Tobago

Constance McTair

ISBN 978-976-8194-75-8

Cover photos: courtesy P.A.T.T.
Design Concept: Constance McTair
Cover and Book Design: Jaime Mungal
Typesetting: Geeta Gobin

Printed and bound in Trinidad and Tobago by RPL (1991) Ltd.
Gulf View Industrial Estate - West,
La Romaine.

Dedication

No vessel can leave port to take passengers and cargo between Trinidad and Tobago without a Master and Chief Engineer.

This account is dedicated to the Masters, Chief Engineers, other officers and crew of the inter-island ferry service – the men and women who have for decades taken us safely across the sea that joins the two main islands of our nation.

The Bocas and the Bulldog

The title of this book comes from the two major
challenges that Masters have faced: negotiating the
turbulent waters of the Trinidad Bocas and steering
clear of Scarborough's treacherous Bulldog Reef.

Contents

Contents

Acknowledgements

Thanks are due to the many present and former port workers who shared their memories with me and generously gave me access to their documents. Special thanks go to Captain Herman Ashton, who introduced me to the Bulldog Reef and who effortlessly recalled dates, names and events from the 1930s to the 1990s - he was an inspiration; and to retired Chief Engineer Desmond Basso, who guided me along the way with words and pictures.

My thanks go as well to retired Comptroller of Customs and Excise, Ralph Newton, and to Dhanlat Mangray, officer in charge of Customs and Excise, Tobago, who told me about Customs laws and regulations.

The staff of the National Archives were immensely helpful, and I must name them – Michael Rivers, Don Johnson, Barry Ahyee, Rawle Chase and Marcelle Thompson. I also want to thank Reginald Dumas for access to his extensive library; Dr. Selwyn Ryan; Captain Lloyd de Roche;

and Theresa Marquez, Sharon Mark and Davidson Hackett of the Port Authority of Trinidad and Tobago (PATT).

Above all, however, I would like to thank Professor Bridget Brereton, who read the manuscript, suggested critical amendments and wrote the foreword, and in particular Noel Garcia, former PATT Chairman, who set me off on this journey of exploration and discovery and without whom this little book would not have seen the light of day.

Foreword

This well-researched history of sea communication between Trinidad and Tobago is both informative and instructive. It is a welcome addition to the historical literature on the two islands.

The development of shipping (of all kinds) is central to Caribbean history, yet it continues to be significantly under-researched by historians and other scholars. This is a region of islands, after all, and from its earliest times the business of getting around by boat helped to shape people's lives. We know the pre-Columbian Amerindians were excellent seafarers, who used their knowledge of boat building and navigation to settle the islands, to trade and raid, and to fish. They taught the arriving Europeans and Africans their techniques and passed on their knowledge of the region and its maritime hazards (our word "hurricane" derived from an Amerindian language).

During the era of slavery, the islands were connected by a lively schooner traffic, often crewed mainly by enslaved or free Africans who developed a high level of seafaring skills. Once slavery had been abolished in the 1830s, there was a large volume of small boat traffic all through the region, taking passengers and cargo, including ex-slaves from the smaller islands like Barbados, Grenada and Tobago going to Trinidad to seek higher wages, and land, in the larger island. We know very little about the history of this schooner traffic of the nineteenth and twentieth centuries: who owned the boats, where were they built and by whom, who crewed them, what was the volume of the traffic, and the typical routes and cargoes. We know more (though still not enough) about international and extra-regional shipping to and from the region, especially the services that connected the colonies to Britain, where documentation is more available.

The sea links between Tobago and Trinidad, especially after they were administratively linked in 1889, are crucial to the economic history of Tobago, especially in the decades after c. 1880 when it became a mainly peasant society, and the export of foodstuffs and livestock to Trinidad was the smaller island's lifeline. Those sea links are also important for an understanding of the volatile political relationship between the two islands. As this book vividly illustrates, nothing soured Tobagonian views about the connection to Trinidad as much as the perennially unsatisfactory state of inter-island sea communications. From the redoubtable A.P.T. James to A.N.R. Robinson and others, the issue has been a major bone of contention.

Constance McTair's study is therefore a valuable contribution to our historical literature and she is to be congratulated.

Bridget Brereton
The University of the West Indies
St. Augustine, Trinidad and Tobago
June 2006

Introduction

While he was Chairman of the Board of the Port Authority of Trinidad and Tobago, Noel Garcia proposed that I write the story of the ferry service. I quickly accepted the challenge. After all, I travel between Trinidad and Tobago only on the ferry. For those of us, like me, who live in Tobago the ferry service is an extension of the country's road system. It is the route that many of us take for advanced medical treatment and education, for entertainment such as attending dance and drama performances, visiting art galleries or going to the cinema, and of course for shopping. It is the route that businesses use for the purchase and delivery of goods. For us the ferry service is very much an essential service.

I leave Tobago at 11 p.m. so my day is not truncated by having to go the airport and wait for a plane that may or may not leave on time, or may not arrive at all from Trinidad. When the plane leaves Crown Point Airport it takes me to Piarco, miles away from where I want to be. My business is in Port of Spain.

To get back to Tobago, I no longer have the option of the occasional 11:00 p.m. sailing, so like all the other driver-passengers I have to line up for hours in the hot sun before being allowed on board. It would take a video documentary to describe this Port of Spain ritual.

However, actual travel on the ferry - in either direction - is a very rewarding experience. I get to hear some very interesting stories etc. I get to hear some interesting stories about politics, the quality of the ferry service, some personal stories told in the most engaging fashion, and news that I never see in the media.

Novelists, short story writers and politicians especially should travel on the ferry.

I do however have to be brutally honest and say that my relationship with the ferry service has not always been rosy. There were times, in the days of manual tickets, when my name and the registration number of my car were not on the manifest although I had confirmed tickets. On those occasions I would have to spend anxious moments trying to find a supervisor to validate my ticket. (The car trunk would be loaded with meat, yoghurt, vegetables and fruit, meaning I would have to get home on time). Was I deleted in Scarborough or Port of Spain? No one could say.

Those of us who travel and transport goods on the ferry are familiar with the stories.

In doing the research for this project I spoke with older passengers and with former and long-serving staff members of the ferry service. They all willingly shared their experiences.

It is because of these encounters that this document goes way back to the 18th century, since it became clear that I needed to put the current service in context. All the same, what I have set down in these pages is not comprehensive. My only hope is that this little contribution to our knowledge of ourselves will convince our institutions of higher learning to pursue further research.

Writing this monograph has been for me a pleasurable and learning experience. Many persons have helped me along the way, but such errors as I may have committed and omissions I may have made are of course my responsibility alone.

Constance McTair
Scarborough, Tobago
Trinidad and Tobago.
compure@tstt.net.tt
May 2006

CHAPTER I

1793 - 1886

In The Beginning

The tug-of-war among Britain, France and the United Provinces of Holland, with Tobago as the rope, had each imperial power claiming victory at intervals. Near the end of the 18th century (February 1, 1793), France declared war on Britain and Holland. With France engaged in naval battles in Europe, the British forces in the West Indies, directed by Henry Dundas, the Secretary of State for the Colonies, recaptured Tobago on April 15, 1793, ending twelve years of French rule of a largely British and African population.[1]

Convinced that Tobago was now firmly British, the planters and merchants immediately started to

---

[1]Britain had ceded Tobago to France in 1783, following French capture of the island in 1781.

agitate for a mail/passenger service in line with that of the British colonies of Barbados and Grenada. Since then, sea transport to and from Tobago has generated strong feelings and impassioned debate on the island.

Through a loose arrangement, the British Imperial Government used the services of private sailing ships to carry official letters and packages to and from its colonies in the West Indies and to receive and deliver the personal mail of its subjects. The shipping company delivered mail to Tobago every two months, but these calls were so short that it was impossible to reply to correspondence before the vessel left the island.

In September 1794, the acting Governor, Joseph Robley, appealed to the Secretary of State for a regular and reliable mail service.

At that time there was no official internal mail delivery service, and planters and merchants had to pay couriers to collect their mail at the only Post Office, which was located in Scarborough. This arrangement was prone to delays since the road system was almost non-existent and the couriers used horses to take them on their route.

The government and people (planters and merchants) of Tobago considered this highly unsatisfactory especially as compared with the more frequent mail calls enjoyed by Grenada and Barbados. Sailing ships delivered mail at St. George's and Bridgetown twice a month. Tobago had earlier asked the shipping company to make a further call on its way to Barbados from Grenada, but these appeals were ignored.

Between the bi-monthly (once every two months) mail calls, the government and residents would pay private schooners to take to Barbados mail and passengers bound for Britain. Sometimes they relied on the kindness of cargo shipping lines to get mail to Barbados.

In his 1794 letter Robley asked that Tobago be placed on an equal footing with Grenada and Barbados. At that time Tobago was part of the Windward Islands government comprising Barbados, Grenada, St. Vincent, St. Lucia and Tobago. The Governor-in-Chief, head of the Windward Islands government, who lived in Barbados, supported Tobago's request. But the bi-monthly mail calls to Tobago continued.

The Barbados intervention "was successful to the extent that three vessels to ply between Tobago and Barbados and carry the mails, were attached to the Tobago Post Office." [2]

---

[2] Archibald, Douglas: *Tobago "Melancholy Isle," Vol. Three,* p. 36

However, this "solution" came at a time when Britain and France were still at war (1799-1814). The three post office vessels were easy targets for French warships and privateers sympathetic to France. They attacked the vessels and captured the mail. The harassment was so intense that the captains and crew of the vessels were given strict orders to dump the mail overboard as soon as they sighted any enemy flags. The purpose was to protect and safeguard official secrets that might be contained in correspondence.

France was untouchable in Europe. Britain ruled the seas and had captured a number of French colonies. The war was at a standoff. Both sides could go no further, so they sat down and agreed on preliminary articles of peace which were confirmed by the Treaty of Amiens on March 27, 1802.[3]

The parties agreed that they would return all the territory that they had captured in the war except Trinidad and Ceylon (Trinidad was ceded by Spain to Britain). Tobago was again French.

Peace was short-lived. In May 1803 Britain and France were again at war. Britain dispatched warships to the southern Caribbean. When the first

---

[3] Tobago, *"Melancholy Isle" Vol. Two,* p.134. Spain and the Batvarian Republic (Holland) also signed the treaty.

4

vessels reached Tobago just as the sun was rising on June 30, 1803, the French Governor offered a bit of face-saving resistance. By nightfall Britain had recaptured Tobago.

But the island did not immediately revert to its former British status. The Imperial Government decided to be cautious; it passed the 1805 "Limitation Act" that denied public funds to captured islands until it was clear which islands were to be ceded and which were to be retained by Britain at war's end.

British sailing ships had stopped their mail and cargo calls during the war and Tobago was again caught in the middle. By 1807, there was little trade, credit was poor, there were foreclosures of mortgages, planters and merchants in Scarborough were impoverished and estates were abandoned.[4]

In 1814 the warring parties signed the Treaty of Paris in which France agreed to cede Tobago to Britain.[5]

After an 11-year break, sailing ships returned to Tobago but mail continued to be delivered on the usual bi-monthly calls. Another 26 years were

---

[4] *Tobago, "Melancholy Isle," Vol. Two,* p.145.
[5] Britain restored all the captured islands to France except for Tobago, St. Lucia and Mauritius.

to pass before the British government entered into a formal arrangement with the newly formed Royal Mail Steam Packet Company (RMSPC), in 1840,[6] for a West Indian mail service in which steamers travelled between the British colonies to take up and land mail.[7]

Under the terms of the contract, steamers had to remain in Tobago for 2 days. Tobago was elated. The Scarborough harbour was upgraded. In 1841 a lighthouse was erected at Bacolet Point (Old Lighthouse Point) by engineers of the militia stationed at Fort King George. The expenditure was approved by the Colonial Office and the Treasury. The lighthouse keeper practised his "3 flashes at intervals of ½ minute" using the oil lamp lighting system. The island awaited the inaugural arrival of the Royal Mail steamer at Scarborough. Tobago was ready for the start of a bright new year - 1842.

But to the consternation of all waiting in the harbour, the captain took the vessel past Scarborough to Great Courland Bay in Plymouth. Tobago merchants and planters were quite unhappy that the RMSPC had insisted on calling at Great

---

[6] RMSPC had been granted a Royal Charter in September 1839.

[7] These steamers also carried passengers and cargo and connected at St. Thomas, Virgin Islands, with the company's trans-Atlantic steamers bound for ports in England.

Courland Bay because in 1841 they had delivered a strongly worded memorandum to the RMSPC representative who had indicated that their vessels would be calling at Plymouth - a town that was 6 miles away from the capital, Scarborough.

The road between Scarborough and Plymouth was a narrow, winding, rough track that made travel difficult. In the dry season, passengers had to contend with the dust. In the rainy season, no one could tell where the road ended and where the river began. Mail and passengers would be delayed. Passengers already wet after coming ashore from the ship in rowboats would have to wait for the water to subside. Then the horses had to be tightly reined in across the mud and slush that masked the danger spots on what passed for a road.

The 1841 memorandum had argued that Plymouth was too far from Scarborough, the capital, that the road between the two towns was almost impassable, and that the island's mercantile interests were being placed in jeopardy. The Lieutenant Governor, Sir Henry Darling, added his endorsement of Scarborough as the port of call over Plymouth.

Nevertheless, on Christmas Eve 1841 the RMSPC told the British Admiralty the Scarborough harbour was fraught with such danger that the company would not risk its vessels in those waters. The Admiralty agreed that Plymouth would be the port of call.[8]

Tobago was not informed.

The Admiralty might have been swayed by an 1810 communication from Governor Hubert Young recommending Scarborough as the seat of government and Plymouth on Courland Bay for the Customs house and "firms of trade."

Young put his case this way:

"... the situation of Plymouth is preferable to that of Scarboro...as a station for shipping,[9] has easier access, better shelter and safer anchorage...Masters of vessels ignorant of the force and direction of the currents in the seas, are often driven to Leeward, to Trinidad or Grenada in making Tobago...or in weathering the eastern headland to fetch Scarboro are hurried on to the Spanish Main..."[10]

The RMSPC steamer did not always land at Plymouth; on occasions it anchored at Little

---

[8] *Tobago, "Melancholy Isle", Vol. Three,* p. 41.

[9] Young was writing when sailing boats brought mail, passengers and cargo.

[10] *Tobago, "Melancholy Isle", Vol. Two,* p. 156.

Courland Bay. Henry Woodcock, then Chief Justice, wrote: "(I)n the absence of anything like competition the Mail Steam Company are despotic in the West Indies, and a mail steamer had often anchored, not at Plymouth, but at Little Courland Bay, about three miles distant from it, exposing passengers to further discomforts and annoyance."[11]

No change to Scarborough came. In his speech at the opening of the Legislative Council (of the Tobago House of Assembly) on September 10, 1850, Lieutenant Governor Dominic Daly said: "It is important in a commercial point of view that rapid communication should exist between this island and the neighbouring Islands, and facilities afforded for Inter-colonial purposes. I congratulate you, therefore, that Tobago has been selected as one of the Termini for the Royal Mail Steam Packet; but I regret to observe, that the Lords of the Admiralty have declined to substitute another Port for Great Courland Bay, for the reception and delivery of Her Majesty's Mails."

Three days later, the vote of thanks to Daly was read into the minutes of the Council meeting. The members of the Council said they were "…at a loss

---

[11] Woodcock, Henry Iles: *A History of Tobago,* pp. 160-1.

to conceive what could have induced the Lords of the Admiralty so pertinaciously to adhere to Courland Bay…after the repeated representations made to them upon that subject, and the easy access of Scarborough Bay…where a Light-House was erected at much cost to the Colony (£828), for the express purpose of enabling the Mails by Steam Packets to be landed with safety."

Meanwhile, the Scarborough harbour was not idle. Large steamships, including those of the very RMSPC, called to load and offload cargo and passengers. Schooners and other small boats carried on a trade in goods between Tobago and Grenada, St. Vincent and Barbados.

In 1852 Daly wrote complaining yet again about the overseas mail service. He said that the Royal Mail boat was often half-way to Trinidad[12] by the time addressees collected their mail at the Scarborough Post Office: "Only in three instances out of fifteen has there been any opportunity of answering letters by the packet that brought them, and that by persons …residing near the post office …"[13]

---

[12] Trinidad was captured from Spain by Britain in 1797 and formally ceded to Britain in 1802.

[13] *Tobago, "Melancholy Isle," Vol. Three*, p. 42.

The Windward Islands Governor-in-Chief (based in Barbados) transmitted the letter to the Secretary of State and supported Daly by stating at the end of his covering letter: "Your Lordship will not be surprised that a great desire is felt that the station of the steamers be changed."

In 1869, 28 years after the lighthouse had been erected and the Scarborough port had been readied and then spurned by the West Indian service of the RMSPC in favour of Great Courland, the British government informed Tobago that it had to pay its share of the cost of bringing mail to the island - £1,361 - if it wanted RMSPC service to continue after that year.

The Speaker of the House of Assembly wrote back to the Secretary of State for the Colonies saying the House was not in the least bit interested in the arrangements between the Imperial Government and the RMSPC: "The repeated refusals of the Royal Mail Co. to land mails at Scarboro render the House indifferent to any arrangements the Imperial Government may make with that company."

The Speaker's tough talk might have taken both the government and the steamship company by surprise because the Tobago Legislative Council heard on March 12, 1872 that the RMSPC would begin a monthly service to Tobago. The port of call would be Scarborough.

The Scarborough harbour was refurbished and the appropriate lights installed. When the new contract started on January 1, 1875, Tobago learned that it was to be served by only one vessel.

The government wanted a more regular service and offered to pay £100 for another monthly mail call, this time from Barbados, but the RMSPC said it was not possible to provide the additional service. The company argued that the small quantity of mail to and from Tobago did not make the additional service economically feasible.

The government meanwhile paid an annual £60 subsidy to the owners of the *Encore* for "the transmission of our bi-weekly (fortnightly) mail to and from Barbados." The service was not reliable.

At the opening of the Legislative Session in 1878, Lieutenant Governor Augustus Frederick Gore told members of the Council "...I am also in communication with the Governor of Trinidad, with a view to establishing a bi-monthly mail between this island and Port of Spain via Arima and Toco."[14]

---

[14] *Tobago, "Melancholy Isle," Vol. Three,* p. 53.

The planters and merchants were frustrated by the inadequacy of sea transport for their goods and in July 1881 a group of Tobago general merchants formed the Tobago Steamship Company. They bought a 100-ton, 20-foot steamer, the *Dawn*, from England, to ply the intra-regional route. The Tobago government granted a £150 annual subsidy for the transport of mail between Tobago and Barbados.[15]

On July 15, 1881 the *Dawn* set out on its first trip from Tobago. The vessel performed well; trade with the islands "was greatly enhanced" for 6½ months. The *Dawn* "opened up considerable intercourse with Trinidad and Grenada."[16]

Tobago was ecstatic.

But on February 10, 1882, the vessel struck a rock at Castara and had to be taken out of service. She was refurbished but never performed well after that accident. Mail began once more to be carried by sailing vessels.

On July 1, 1885 the Imperial Government signed a new contract with the RMSPC in which steamers of the West Indian service were required to call at Scarborough once every 4 weeks after handling mail at St. Vincent, Grenada, Trinidad and

[15] Ottley, C.R. *The Island of Tobago, British West Indies,* p. 127.
[16] *Tobago, "Melancholy Isle", Vol. Three,* p.56.
[17] *Tobago, "Melancholy Isle", Vol. Three,* p.57.

Barbados. The vessels were to stay in the harbour for a 6-day layover. The crew played games in the street during the layover and complained about the absence of street lights at night.[17]

About 1886 Messrs. Scrutton, Sons & Co. of London sent their ships to Tobago to load sugar and other cargo. The colonial government of Trinidad and Tobago paid no subsidy for the service and it was discontinued about four years later.

Messrs Gillespie & Co., which owned many Tobago estates, also regularly sent steamers to Tobago in the 1880s to load sugar, rum and molasses.

Meanwhile, the Colonial Office was contemplating Tobago's administrative fate.

Royal Mail Steamer in Scarborough Bay (1900)
Courtesy: Miles Almandoz.

CHAPTER II

1887 - 1927

Trinidad and Tobago united
to form one colony

The Trinidad and Tobago Act (of the UK Parliament) 1887, provided that "Her Majesty is empowered by Order in Council to declare that the Colony of Trinidad and the Colony of Tobago shall, from a date to be mentioned in such Order, be united into and form one Colony on such terms and conditions as Her Majesty should, in such Order in Council, or in any subsequent Order or Orders, think fit to appoint...."

On November 28, 1888, an Order in Council uniting the colony of Trinidad and its dependencies and the colony of Tobago to form the Colony of Trinidad and Tobago was gazetted. The effective date of the unification was January 1, 1889. The powers and functions of the Governor-in-Chief of the Windward Islands in respect of Tobago ceased on December 31, 1888. In addition, the powers and functions of the Executive and Legislative Councils of Tobago ceased to exist on the same day.

An April 6, 1889 Order in Council made changes to the original Order of unification but this Order was itself later revoked by Order in Council of October 20, 1898.

The 1898 Order revoked all the clauses of the original Order in Council except for clauses 1, 2 and 37. Clause 1 had declared the date of unification as January 1, 1889. The Order also declared Tobago a ward, i.e., an administrative district, of the colony of Trinidad and Tobago.

Sea Transport between the islands of Trinidad and Tobago

The abolition of slavery and apprenticeship (1834-1838) and the almost total collapse of estate production in Tobago led to the formation of a new class, i.e., the peasant farmer. The former slaves and their descendants either squatted on or bought lands (a few were given land grants) and began producing for internal and external markets. It was this group that was to rely most heavily on safe and reliable sea communication from Tobago.

One of the first acts of the colonial government of Trinidad and Tobago related to sea transport. A contract had earlier been signed with Turnbull Stewart & Co. of Trinidad[18] for a coastal steamer service around Trinidad en route to New York. The colonial government added Tobago to the route and from the start of the service in 1889 Tobago began to enjoy a fortnightly service.

The main purpose of the government contract with Turnbull Stewart was to encourage an export trade in bananas and citrus with the United States. Turnbull Stewart received an annual subsidy of £5,000 for 7 years using the 350-ton *Victoria,* then the 160-ton *Magnetic,* on the route. "The export trade did not materialise and after a few years the subsidy to the steamship service was withdrawn."[19]

Also beginning in 1889 was a coastal steamer service to Trinidad's east and north-east bays. In October of that year service to Scarborough was added to the route of the *s.s. Bel Air,* one of the Trinidad coastal steamers.[20]

---

[18] Turnbull Stewart were also contractors for an island steam service that called at Port of Spain, Carenage, Five Islands, Carrera, Gasparee and Monos (Collens, J.H., *Guide to Trinidad,* p. 237).

[19] Brereton, Bridget: *A History of Modern Trinidad, 1783-1962,* pp. 95-6.

[20] Handbook of Trinidad and Tobago 1889.

In 1896 Ellis Grell and Co. started to receive an annual subsidy of £4,200 to run a coastal service along the Gulf of Paria with calls at Scarborough 42 times each year. The company first ran the steamer *Pioneer* on the route, followed by the *Manzanares*, but the service was erratic.

The government attempted to supplement the *Manzanares* run with a contract to ship mail to Tobago from Toco in a small sailing boat, but the waters on Trinidad's north coast were unforgiving. The sailing boat had to abandon the voyage on many occasions. That contract was very quickly terminated.

The government contracts the RMSPC to run the coastal service

The subsidy to Ellis Grell and Co. ended when the government entered its first 5-year contract (1901-1906) with the RMSPC for a weekly steamship service along the coastal bays in Trinidad and around Tobago. The company received an annual subsidy of £7,000 and was required to make 42 calls to Scarborough each year.

The Trinidad service began on March 19, 1901; the Tobago service started 6 months later (September).[21]

The RMSPC ran two boats. The 470-ton *Spey* arrived in October 1901, travelled around Tobago and called at Port of Spain weekly. The *Kennet* – 827 tons – had arrived in March. This vessel made a weekly call at Scarborough after travelling around Trinidad.

The *Spey* and the *Kennet* continued on the routes for another 5 years (1906-1911) with an increased annual subsidy of £7,250 that required the vessels to give Scarborough three additional calls (45 calls per year).

The *Belize* and the *Barima*

The RMSPC replaced the *Spey* and the *Kennet* with larger vessels in 1911. The *Belize* and the *Barima*, each of 1500 tonnage, added another call to Scarborough. The subsidy remained at £7,250 per annum for the larger vessels.

The *Belize* was specially built by the RMSPC to provide a subsidised service around the coasts of Trinidad and Tobago.[22] But it was the *Belize* that travelled around Tobago while the *Barima* went

---

[21] The RMSPC West Indian service that connected Tobago with Grenada and Barbados continued to call at Scarborough until 1905.

[22] Handbook of Trinidad and Tobago 1924.

around the Trinidad Atlantic coast. Each vessel called at Scarborough.

The Trinidad and Tobago Legislative Council met in extraordinary session on December 12, 1915 following the RMSPC announcement that the *Barima* was to be pulled out of service because the British Government needed vessels for the war effort during World War I (1914-18).

The Acting Colonial Secretary moved: "That this Council approves of the proposal of the Royal Mail Steam Packet Company ... for a modification of the Coastal Service Contract ... so as to provide that the service shall for the remainder of the contract be performed by one steamer instead of two, and the annual subsidy reduced from £7,250 to £3,265."

The *Barima* was pulled out of service in 1916, leaving the *Belize* to service both Tobago and Trinidad.[23] Tobago merchants, planters and the growing peasant class vigorously protested the loss of their dedicated *Belize* service. No replacement came for the *Barima* and there is no evidence that it was ever used in the war effort.

---

[23] The RMSPC then received an annual subsidy of £5,000 for the *Belize*. This was later reduced to £3,250.

The colonial government renewed its contract with the RMSPC in 1916 for the *Belize* to continue the service on Trinidad's Atlantic coast and the coasts of Tobago with stops in Scarborough. But Tobago was not satisfied with the company's performance. The *Belize* was often delayed and at times there was no service at all.

The government now had to deal with irate travellers and business interests in both Tobago and Trinidad. The RMSPC claimed to be running at a loss while the government thought that the service the colony was getting was not commensurate with the high cost of the subsidy paid.

In 1923 the government acquired 2 small vessels - the 183-ton *St. Patrick*,[24] which carried 250 passengers, and the 94-ton *Naparima* with a passenger load of 200. The vessels were placed on the *Icacos Service* and the *Bocas Service*. The Icacos Service called at San Fernando, La Brea-Brighton, Guapo, Cap-de-Ville, Irois Forest, Granville and Cedros,[25] bays on the Gulf of Paria coast. The *Bocas Service* travelled to the Five Islands (see map - next page).

---

[24] By 1930, the *St. Patrick* was running both *Gulf* and *Bocas* services: Monday to Wednesday it served the *Bocas* and fulfilled its regular *Gulf* schedule for the remainder of the week.

[25] Handbook of Trinidad and Tobago 1924, p. 118.

21

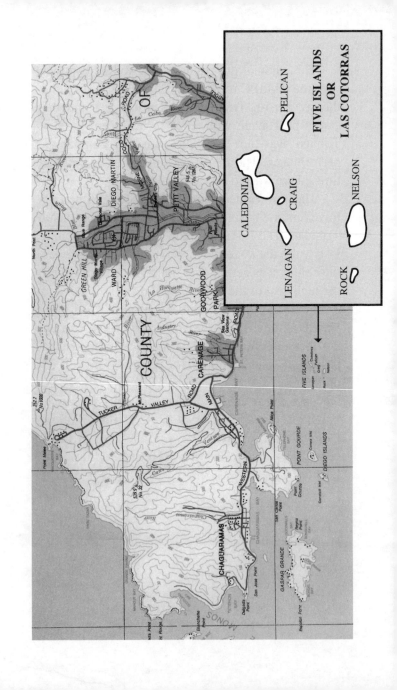

The Belize in Port of Spain

s.s. Paria travelled to the Five Islands
Photo: courtesy Gerry Besson.

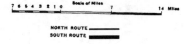

MAP OF
TRINIDAD AND TOBAGO
SHOWING COASTAL STEAMER ROUTE.

Scale of Miles
7 6 5 4 3 2 1 0   7   14 Miles

NORTH ROUTE ——————
SOUTH ROUTE ▬▬▬▬▬

CARIBBEAN

Blanchisseuse

Blanchisseuse

Huevos
Chacachacare
Patos
Monos
Gasparee
Teteron

Diego Martin

St. Ann's
PORT-OF-SPAIN

ST. GEORGE
Tacarigua   Arima
                Arima

Caroni

Cunupia

Chaguanas

CARONI

Couva

Montserrat

Tabaquite   Charu

Pointe-à-Pierre
Pointe-à-Pierre

San Fernando

TRINIDAD

GULF OF PARIA

La Brea
Pt. Fortin   Guapo
La Brea
Cap de Ville
Granville
Cedros
Chatham
Isacos   Erin   Palo Seco
Erin Bay

Naparima

Princes Town

Savana Grande

VICTORIA
Ortoire

ST. PATRICK Siparia Siparia

Erin

Moruga

Moruga

Belize route map presented to the 1928 Murphy Sea Committee by the Habour Master

In March 1923 the colonial government purchased the *Belize* outright for £24,000 (a little less than the cost of 3 years of subsidy), but a further expenditure of £6,693 went on re-conditioning the vessel.

The government then appointed Messrs. Alston and Co. Ltd. as their agents.

A new type of contract was drawn up between the parties. The government moved away from subsidies, and Alston & Co. Ltd. had to manage and maintain the coastal service between Trinidad and Tobago for 7½% of earnings. Under the terms of the agreement, Scarborough had to continue to enjoy 46 calls each year.

The company fulfilled its contract with a weekly coastal steamer service going every alternate week by the northern and southern routes.

On the northern route it took 18 hours to get from Port of Spain to Scarborough. The *Belize* left Port of Spain for Blanchisseuse at 9 p.m. on Monday. Then it was on to Grande Riviere, Matelot and Toco before sailing to Scarborough to load and offload passengers and cargo at 3 p.m. on Tuesday. It was then time to move on to do the same at 11 bays around Tobago. The 12th bay was Bloody Bay, which received a call every other Thursday. The round-Tobago stops took almost 2 days.

For the return trip, the vessel left Scarborough at 8 p.m. on Thursday for the 2½ hour voyage to Toco, from where she sailed directly to Port of Spain arriving at 6 a.m. on Friday. The vessel was therefore at sea for 81 hours.

On the following Monday, loaded with passengers and cargo, the *Belize* would set off for Tobago on the southern route.[26]

On this route the vessel would take 48 hours to get to Scarborough from Port of Spain. She would leave Port of Spain at 6 p.m. on Monday for Pointe-a-Pierre to take on bunker fuel. Then it was on through the Serpent's Mouth to Moruga, Guayaguayare, St Margaret's, St. Ann's, Plaisance and St. Joseph, arriving in Scarborough at 6 p.m. on Wednesday. On her return from Scarborough (12 noon on Thursday), the vessel stopped at Toco, Sans Souci, Matelot, Grande Riviere and Blanchisseuse, and arrived in Port of Spain on Friday at 6 p.m.

There were 4 categories of tickets – 1st class, 2nd class, 3rd class and excursion 1st class. Return tickets were valid for three months but one-way tickets were valid only for the trip for which they were issued. There were no weekend sailings.

---

[26] All the stops between Port of Spain and Scarborough and those around Tobago were legally classified as "sufferance wharves". See glossary.

Belize Fares

Class	One Way £. s. d.[27]	Return £. s. d.
1st class excursion	-----	3. 2. 6
1st class	1. 5. 0	2. 0. 0
2nd class	- 12. 6	1 0. 0
3rd class	- 6. 3	- 10. 0

The price of a return excursion 1st class ticket included meals.

Alston & Co. Ltd managed the ferry service on behalf of the government from March 1923 to June 1927.

In December 1924 the *s.s. Belize* grounded on the rocks off Petit Trou Bay, Trinidad. "The ship was considered to be in a dangerous position on account of the heavy surf that was running, and the passengers numbering between 40 and 50 were all safely landed at Toco in the surf boats, and brought into Port of Spain by motor buses."[28]

---

[27] Pounds, shillings and pence. Rate of exchange: £ 1 = $4.80; 1s = 24cts; 1d = 2cts.

[28] Harbour Master's report to the Colonial Secretary dated August 15, 1936.

The vessel had to be docked for 132 consecutive days to repair the damage.

During that time, sloops became once again the only means of sea transport between Trinidad and Tobago. The government arranged for a fortnightly call by Canadian National Steamships on their north and south trips to and from Demerara (British Guiana) pending the return of the Belize.

Between 1917 and 1927, the *s.s. Belize* did not sail for a total of 330 days. The steamer either was dry docked or was being overhauled or was subject to "frequent, sudden and protracted interruption."

CHAPTER III

1927 - 1937

The Beginning of the Government Shipping Service

On July 1, 1927 the colonial government took over full control of the coastal steamer service through the Harbour Master's office. This was the beginning of the government shipping service.

By this time, the cost of refits, insurance, dry docking and repairs of the *Belize* was mounting each year.

Tobago merchants, peasant farmers and traffickers were complaining loudly about the inadequacy of the vessel for the agricultural and commercial requirements of the island and about the damage being done to their cargo on board the vessel and at the wharf in Port of Spain.

Losses were also being regularly reported. There was mounting dissatisfaction.

The 1928 Sea Communication Committee

On May 15, 1928 the government appointed the Sea Communication Committee under the chairmanship of the Director of Public Works, M.A. Murphy, C.B.E:

> "to make enquiry as to how the sea communication needs of Tobago may be most economically and satisfactorily provided for after the establishment of the steamship service contemplated by the Canada-West Indies Trade Agreement of 1925" and "to advise whether a satisfactory scheme calculated to meet the needs of both Tobago and the Coastal Service of Trinidad can be drawn up, having due regard to the possibility of a fuller utilization of the road system both in Tobago and Trinidad."

The Harbour Master, a member of the committee, moaned: "In spite of the extensive refit in 1927 the cost of repairs (to the *Belize*) in 1928 was £2,800 and it is, I fear, now evident that the annual expenditure for repairs will be considerably increased."[29]

---

[29] Report to the 1928 Sea Communication Committee.

In his appearance before the committee, the Master of the *Belize* asked for a decrease in the number of bays where the vessel was required to call. "Plymouth and Milford have both ceased to be of any value...Bloody Bay...is a totally unnecessary call...Pembroke could be done away with...Hillsborough definitely..." He also suggested that certain stops on the Trinidad coast should be eliminated.[30]

The frequent stops around the islands on the north trip caused the vessel to leave Scarborough behind schedule, sometimes 24 hours late. The Master argued that if the number of calls was reduced the steamer would run on time and an additional call could be made at Scarborough.

Harold Joseph Kernahan, manager of several estates in the Leeward District of Tobago, told the committee that the *Belize* could not account for "6,000 bags" of his produce each year.

In its report the committee recommended taking the *Belize* out of service and placing two smaller boats on the route.

The committee also declared: "This service constitutes the only link apart from a few sloops

---

[30] The January 7, 1932 *Gazette* gave notice of the closure of the coastal steamer depot at Moruga on January 30, 1932 - "Steamers will not call at Moruga after that date except by special arrangement."

which Tobago has with the outside world. It must therefore be regarded as a public utility service…" The committee noted further that the steamship service contemplated by the Canada-West Indies Trade Agreement of 1925 placed no obligation on the Canadian government to provide steamer communication to Tobago. [31]

Before the committee's recommendations could be implemented, Tobago clergymen, merchants and planters met on September 11, 1929, and agreed to send a telegram to the Secretary of State for the Colonies asking for an immediate inquiry. The text of the telegram was delivered to the acting Governor of Trinidad and Tobago for transmission to the Secretary of State. The telegram read:

"We respectfully request immediate inquiry into isolated condition of Tobago and ruinous interference with trade, business, postal arrangements due to neglect on part of the department responsible in removing local steamer from route without adequate notice of any previous provision

---

[31] Between 1899 and 1904 the Imperial and Canadian governments each contributed an annual subsidy of £13,500 to Pickford & Black steamers for service between Canada and the West Indies. Tobago received a few monthly calls.

for carrying on regular passenger, mail or freight service during absence of steamer. No prospect of travelling from Trinidad to Tobago for several weeks. Local Government apparently helpless."

The acting Governor sent the telegram with his comments on September 13. He told the Secretary of State:

"Owing to urgent need of overhauling engines and docking local steamer *Belize*, our local dock having been reported unsafe it was found necessary to lay *Belize* at short notice and to send her to Martinique for docking. Best arrangements possible have been made to arrange for transport of mails, passengers and cargo to and from Tobago by motor and sailing vessels but such services are necessarily irregular and uncertain.

"Subsequent to *Belize* being laid up Canadian National Steamships have inaugurated a four-weekly cargo service calling at Tobago north and south bound on way to and from Trinidad and Demerara

35

and I have arranged for a fortnightly service pending return of the *Belize*. The latter arrangement was only concluded subsequent to receipt of the above message. Despatch follows."

Five days later, the acting Governor sent his despatch (report) in which he said:

"I must admit that I have considerable sympathy with the complaint from Tobago where regular steamer communications have been interrupted by the docking of the *Belize*. The *Belize* has to be withdrawn for the purpose twice a year, and it is not always possible to replace her while she is in dock by chartering another vessel to maintain the service. The inconvenience which the people of Tobago undoubtedly suffer on these occasions is likely to be a frequent occurrence as long as only one vessel is employed for maintaining a steamer service between Trinidad and Tobago...

"In view of the enquiry which has already been made into the existing situation by the Tobago Sea Communication Committee and of the action which is being taken as a result of the Committee's recommendation, I do not consider that any useful purpose would be served by arranging for any further enquiry."

The acting Governor also informed the Secretary of State that the Tobago Sea Communication Committee had recommended the purchase of two steamers of lesser tonnage to replace the *Belize* and that the Crown Agents had been asked to provide the cost of suitable vessels.[32]

Meanwhile, private enterprise sought to bring relief to passengers and to provide cargo space. F.S. Bansta of South Quay, Port of Spain, and Scarborough placed an advertisement in the March 13, 1930 edition of the *Gazette* offering "attractive freight and passage rates" on the motor schooner *Grenville Lass* which "will maintain a regular weekly cargo and deck passenger service between P.O.S. and Scarborough and certain outports[33] of Tobago, leaving P.O.S. every Monday at 6 p.m. and arriving back at P.O.S. at daylight on Friday."

---

[32] Colonial Office document CO295/567/9 contains the acting Governor's report dated September 18, 1929 and the text of the September 13 telegram.

[33] The vessel called at Pembroke, Roxborough, Mt Irvine and Milford on alternate weeks.

The *s.s. Tobago* and the *s.s. Trinidad*

The government later received two coastal steamers specially built for conditions in the coastal waters of Trinidad and Tobago.

The steamers were the 500-ton *s.s. Tobago* which arrived in January 1931 and the 600-ton *s.s. Trinidad* which came a few months later. The vessels did not have the long itinerary of the *Belize*; travel time between Port of Spain and Scarborough was so drastically reduced that on April 20, 1931, the *Tobago* left Port of Spain on its 16th trip.

Passengers were now enjoying 9-hour trips between Port of Spain and Scarborough and an 8-hour journey between Scarborough and Port of Spain.

The *Tobago* and the *Trinidad* offered a passenger and cargo service on alternate days with a return service on intervening days. Normally, each vessel made three round trips each week, giving Tobago, for the first time, an almost daily service between the islands. The vessels left both ports at night.[34]

---

[34] The *Belize* continued to call at ports on Trinidad's Atlantic coast until she was decommissioned in the early 1930s.

A typical week's sailing schedule was as follows:[35]

Day of the week	s.s. *Trinidad*	s.s. *Tobago*
Monday	Docked in POS	Departs POS 9:00 p.m.
Tuesday	Departs POS 9:00 p.m.	Departs Scarborough 10:00 p.m.
Wednesday	Departs Scarborough 10:00 p.m.	Departs POS 9:00 p.m.
Thursday	Departs POS 9:00 p.m.	Departs Scarborough 10:00 p.m.
Friday	Departs Scarborough 10:00 p.m.	Departs POS 9:00 p.m.
Saturday	Departs POS 9:00 p.m.	Departs Scarborough 10:00 p.m.
Sunday	Departs Scarborough 10:00 p.m.	Docked in POS

The vessels usually crossed each other around 1 a.m. and arrived at their respective ports at 6:00 a.m. The following week the ships changed schedule.

---

[35] During the Second World War, in the period 1942 – 1944, German U boats attacked vessels in the Caribbean. The north coast was known as 'torpedo junction', and no vessel ventured out at night. (Ulric Cross, *The History of Aviation in Trinidad and Tobago – 1915-1962,* p.86)
The Tobagonian, October 1944, records that during the war the coastal vessels sailed during the day.

On alternate Fridays the *s.s. Trinidad* remained in Trinidad for the loading of cargo for Scarborough and the coastal bays of Tobago.

The following Monday night she set out for Scarborough, arriving there around 6 a.m. to discharge cargo. Three hours later she was off to Roxborough, the first stop on her round-the-island trip, to off-load and collect passengers and cargo. Then it was on the next bay and the next as she sailed along the windward and leeward coasts, finally returning to Scarborough around 6 a.m. on Friday morning to get ready for a 10.00 p.m. departure for Port of Spain. On this voyage - three days and four nights around Tobago - the return fare was $15.00 (exclusive of meals).

The Master of the *Belize* had complained in 1928 about the frequent stops his vessel had to make around the islands.

There was no complaint from the Master and crew of the *Trinidad* about their calls at Tobago bays. It was for them an excursion, although the stops continued to involve arduous work by the stevedores, who first had to off-load cargo from the steamer to 'Moses' (surf/bum) boats, then assist the ladies as they climbed down the rope ladders to enter the boats, which would sail as close to shore as possible. Then the stevedores, with water sometimes reaching close to their armpits depending on the tide, would lift the heavy sacks of flour, rice, etc on their shoulders and heads to take them to the shore.

Gentlemen that they were, the stevedores also carried to shore the women, some of them rather buxom, draped over their shoulders. As might be expected, the stevedores rather enjoyed this exercise. Male passengers generally had to fend for themselves.

If there were passengers and cargo to be loaded at the bay then it was time for the reverse action of lifting the cargo (and the ladies, of course) across the water to the surf boats from which the gentlemen-stevedores ensured that the ladies climbed the rungs of the ladder to the safety of the vessel. Then it was on to the next bay to repeat the process.

Revenue exceeds expenditure

By the end of 1937, the traffic on the coastal steamers was so heavy that revenue exceeded expenditure for the first time in the history of the coastal steamer service. And little wonder, because the vessels were carrying much more than their prescribed loads on long holiday weekends and during school vacations (pcak periods).

In addition, at mid-week traffickers and farmers carried their produce to trade on the POS wharf or at the market in Port of Spain.

The vessels were built for the following passenger loads:

Vessel	1st class	2nd class	3rd class	Cars
s.s. Tobago	18	14	60	2
s.s. Trinidad	18	12	90	2

Official figures presented to the 1938 Nicholl Committee (see Chapter IV) showed that the vessels were carrying almost three times the recommended number of passengers at peak periods and midweek.

Weekend and midweek passenger loads[36]

Vessel	1st class	2nd class	3rd class	Cars
s.s. Tobago	28	26	150-180	2
s.s. Trinidad	28	26	150-180	2

In addition, 95% of Tobago's exports moved on the steamers.

---

[36] The 1957 Wharton Commission of Inquiry found these figures understated.

Overload or not, the government believed that the sea communication service should be a revenue earner. To do this, special weekend excursion fares were offered.[37] To encourage travel during the "low season", special rates applied. And a return fare of $6.00 was available for travel between Friday and Tuesday (the regular return fare was $10.00).

To earn even more revenue, the government took the steamers off the route for excursions to British Guiana, Barbados and Grenada to collect cargo and also to transport tourists between ship and shore when tourist ships visited Port of Spain. Passengers were left stranded and trade between the islands was affected. Merchants, farmers, small businessmen and women, traffickers, holiday seekers all complained, and the Government quickly reversed itself, discontinuing the pattern of using the vessels for purposes other than the transport of passengers and cargo between Trinidad and Tobago.

---

[37] Ottley, C.R. *The Island of Tobago, British West Indies,* p.13.

The Harbour Master and the Customs offices shared this building in Port of Spain. Fire destroyed the building in 1979.

Photos: courtesy Miles Almandoz.

CHAPTER IV

1938 - 1950

The 1938 Sea Communication Committee

In April 1938 another sea communication committee (the Nicholl Committee) was appointed "to advise the government whether the existing coastal steamer service between Trinidad and Tobago is adequate for the present needs; and if the existing service is not considered satisfactory, to make recommendations with a view to its improvement in the light of present circumstances and probable developments in the future."

The committee held meetings in Tobago and Trinidad and received memoranda from interested parties such as the Tobago Chamber of Commerce, the Harbour Master, the Masters of the *Trinidad* and the *Tobago* and the veterinary officer, Tobago.

In the preamble to its report of June 15, the committee said:

"As transport is essentially ancillary to the economic life of the area which it serves we found it necessary to place a wide interpretation on our terms of reference... We wish to make it clear at the outset that, if substantial expenditure is to be incurred on improving transport facilities for Tobago, such expenditure can only be justified if a vigorous policy of economic development is pursued both by the government and the people of Tobago."

Tobago's exports to Trinidad had been increasing since 1933. The value of exports had moved from $394,382.70 in 1935 to $594,653.95 in 1936.

The following is taken from the table of exports on the steamers for the period 1933 to 1937.[38]

Tobago Exports, 1936-1937
Quantity And Value

		1936		1937	
Article	**Unit**	**Quantity**	**Value** **$. c**	**Quantity**	**Value** **$. c**
Cattle	Head	758	22,740.00	688	20,640.00
Fowls	Dozen	2,375	11,970.00	2,202	12,683.52
Cocoa	Lb.	3,017,092	305,340.09	2,079,299	176,740.41
Copra	Lb.	4,991,853	137,969.80	6,342,496	190,274.88
Fruit(mixed)	Lb.	282,665	2,620.05	936,278	2,362.78
Limes	Lb.	69,655	966.15	109,470	1,094.70
Tobacco	Lb.	59,032	6,563.26	58,059	11,611.80

These figures do not include the cargo that was shipped on sloops.

Some producers who could afford it preferred to ship by sloop. They argued that their goods reached Port of Spain with less spoilage or loss. They also claimed that the sloop owners readily refunded them for loss, unlike the managers at the port.

---

[38] Document attached to the report of the 1938 Nicholl Sea Communication Committee, Appendix B.

In its report, the 1938 Sea Communication Committee advised the Government that the sea service did not meet the requirements of the existing traffic:

"...(p)assenger traffic between Trinidad and Tobago consists of residents of Tobago and tourists, i.e., travellers from overseas and holiday makers from Trinidad. ...The accommodation for 3rd class passengers is most unsatisfactory. Seating accommodation is lacking, and the majority of 3rd class passengers perforce have to sit or lie on the deck."

The committee found the boat service and boat landing for passengers at Scarborough to be also unsatisfactory.[39]

It expressed concern about the arrangement for handling cargo including live animals, and called for immediate improvement in the method used, particularly at Scarborough, to load livestock on the vessels. Cargo including live animals was first

---

[39] At that time steamers anchored in the stream (a few hundred yards from the shore). Passengers had to take privately-owned rowboats or the surf boats to get to and from the shore.

placed in what may be described as crates then loaded on lighters and taken close to the steamers. The crates were lifted by derricks and loaded on board the vessel.

The committee made a number of recommendations that covered tourism, agriculture, marketing, road development and an improved sea communication service. On sea communication, it recommended *inter alia* that:

- a regular and uninterrupted steamer service be established

- a protected boat landing at Scarborough be constructed and a Government boat service between ship and shore be established

- a new ship be purchased which would be capable of maintaining a 5-hour-alternate-day-daylight passenger service between Port of Spain and Scarborough. It should carry at least 5 motor cars and be equipped with a certain amount of cold storage for perishable freight

- the new vessel should also be equipped
  with wireless for the transmission of
  emergency messages

- the *s.s. Trinidad* be employed mainly
  as a cargo carrier but also maintain a
  night passenger service once a week
  each way. The vessel should be
  modified to provide good
  accommodation for livestock

- the *s.s. Tobago* be a reserve ship which
  should also be used to open up trade
  with other Caribbean islands.

The committee also called for a fast daylight
vessel because it argued that "…to provide a night
service with its essential cabin accommodation
… a large ship would be required and, as the cost
of passages must bear relation to the cost of the
service, passage costs necessarily would be high…
It is appreciated that a fast ship is costly to run…"

But the *Trinidad* and *Tobago* continued to run
until early 1957, giving almost 26 years' service
under trying circumstances.

Air Service

The challenge to passenger sea transport came when commercial airline transport between the islands started nearly three and a half years after the Nicholl report. On November 27, 1941[40] BWIA opened connections between Trinidad, Tobago and Barbados.

Captain Mikey Cipriani, a Trinidadian athlete, lawyer and World War I soldier, wanted to establish a mail service flight between Trinidad and Tobago. On a cloudy June 3, 1934, Cipriani flew out on course for Shirvan Park, Tobago but his plane crashed in the Northern Range and he was killed. Hopes for the transport of mail by air were dashed but were revived five years later when Jack St. Hilaire successfully completed a flight in memory of Cipriani on June 4, 1939, opening the air route between Trinidad and Tobago.[41]

Meanwhile, the government was again expressing concern over the rising cost of maintaining the steamer service, which was being run at a loss of $20,000 yearly.

---

[40] Tobago's first aerodrome at Fort Milford was completed in 1941-42. The first flights from Trinidad to Tobago were on the sea-planes, the first of which landed off Plymouth on May 8, 1930. Flights lasted 35 minutes. (Ulric Cross, *The History of Aviation in Trinidad and Tobago 1915-1962*, p. 24).

[41] Cross, *op. cit.*, p. 52.

s.s. Tobago in Scarborough - 1950
Photo courtesy: Miles Almandoz

CHAPTER V

1951 - 1957

The 1951 Sea Communication Committee

The Select Committee on the 1951 Estimates recommended the appointment of a yet another committee to examine the operations of the service. The government accepted the recommendation and named the members of the committee in August 1951. The Chairman was A. W. Baddeley and its terms of reference were:

"to investigate the working of the coastal Steamer and Island Launch Services and the system of communication between Trinidad and Tobago and to make recommendations with a view to reducing the annual deficits incurred on both of these services."

Tobago's interests were represented by A.P.T. James, Tobago representative on the Legislative

Council, and T.C. Cambridge, former public servant, historian and curator of the Tobago Museum. The Secretary of the committee was J.F. Belle, a senior public officer from Tobago.

The committee submitted two (2) interim reports and its recommendations to reduce the annual deficits on the coastal steamer included:

- an increase in the first-class return fare from $12.00 to $14.40 [42]

- higher freight rates [43]

- introduction of a return fare for 2nd and 3rd class passengers - double the single fare less 10% [44]

- low increases for the transport of fruits, vegetables and groceries

- increased freight charges of 2 cents on a 100lb bag of flour; 5 cents on a 180lb bag of rice; and 2½ cents on a 100lb bag of sugar.

---

[42] The return airfare between Trinidad and Tobago was the same - $14.40.

[43] Freight rates were last increased on June 1, 1948.

[44] 2nd and 3rd class single fares were to remain the same.

"…These increases should have very little effect on the cost of living in Tobago," the committee declared.

The committee also recommended an end to the fortnightly direct service between Scarborough and Roxborough. In 1950, the *Trinidad* made 25 direct trips from Scarborough to Roxborough at a cost of approximately $50,000; the revenue earned on these trips totalled $4,250.

As for the "courtesy" calls at the Hermitage estate to pick up mail, the committee said it could see "no justification for the continuance of this call particularly when it is borne in mind that the proprietors at Anse Fourmi have to transport their produce for 3½ miles by boat to Bloody Bay."

Hermitage estate [45] is located about 1½ miles west of Charlotteville but there was an arrangement with the estate owner by which he would hoist a signal flag on the beach to indicate that he needed to send an item or items on the steamer. It might have been just one letter but once that flag was planted, the vessel had to call at the Hermitage Bay.

The committee called for the acquisition of two (2) new vessels of 600 and 500 gross tons and the maintaining of three (3) round trips

---

[45] The Hermitage Estate is now owned by the Fernandes family.

between the islands every week:

"This service is considered adequate for cargo purposes. However, as in most cross-channel services the vessels are congested with passengers during weekend and holiday periods."

In his appearance before the committee, the Director of Works and Hydraulics had explained that Part V of the Five-Year Economic Programme referred to a proposed $400,000 road from Castara to Bloody Bay, but the item fell under the heading "Matters to receive further consideration." This meant that construction of the northside road might or might not be a part of that Programme although the decision-makers were aware that those communities were cut off from the rest of the island.

Just one year before the Governor, Sir Hubert Rance, had spent eleven days in Tobago. In his July 5, 1950 account of his visit to the Colonial Secretary, Rance wrote in part:

"...The main grouses of the Tobagonian were, no electric light...lack of roads ... and communication facilities for certain villages on the North East coast. ...All of these grouses are well founded.

"The three small villages on the North East Coast each with a population of 300 are a serious problem. Two of them are cut off from the outside world except by sea and the third is approachable only by a jeep track which I traversed in a jeep and can vouch that it was the most hazardous trip I have ever undertaken, not excepting Burma."[46]

In its October 1951 report the Sea Communication Committee urged the government to place Tobago's road development among the matters scheduled for completion within the first five-year period:

"The committee recognises that the round-Tobago service contributes largely to the present loss... (but) the proposal for the discontinuance of this service can only be pursued (on the completion) of the North Coast Road."

---

[46] Colonial Office reference CO 295/651.

Scarborough port improvement

Around this time the Scarborough port was being upgraded so that steamers could berth alongside the wharf.

For decades passengers had had to pay boatmen to take them to and from the steamers which anchored in the stream; or, if they had the patience, they would wait on the vessels' surf boats that carried passengers and cargo to and from the shore.

The boatmen carried on a very competitive business. The Harbour Master was very unhappy with their behaviour, their arbitrary pricing and their exploitation of passengers.

The government attempted to bring the situation under control by publishing the Harbours Ordinance, Chapter 118 in the *Trinidad Royal Gazette* on September 17, 1931. The publication contained "Regulations and Table of Boat Fares for the Harbour of Scarborough":

> "All boats shall lie off steamers and other vessels carrying passengers at a distance of not less than twenty yards except as hereinafter directed.

"Not more than one boat shall be allowed to come alongside a steamer or other vessel at the same time for the purpose of taking in or embarking passengers and their luggage, and shall not be permitted to remain longer than is actually necessary.

"No boatman shall in any boat lying within twenty yards alongside of any steamer or other vessel carrying passengers

Be drunk and disorderly; or

Make use of any violent or obscene language with intent to provoke any person to commit a breach of the peace; or

Use any obscene or profane language to the annoyance of any person; or

Fight or otherwise disturb the peace."

The boatmen blithely ignored the regulations because the 1938 Sea Communication Committee reported that there was indiscipline at the Scarborough port.[47]

The 1931 Harbours Ordinance also set the boat fares for coastal steamer passengers who each had a baggage allowance "including such small articles as the passenger may carry in his hand, and two ordinary packages of luggage":

From sunrise to sunset	4d
From sunset to sunrise	6d
Sundays and Public Holidays	6d
Baggage: For every package beyond the above	3d

A higher fare was set for those who came to Tobago on vessels other than the coastal steamers.

Boatmen at the Scarborough harbour became redundant when the 490ft wharf was formally

---

[47] Later Commissions were horrified by the indiscipline of passengers in Port of Spain and Scarborough.

opened on January 28, 1953.[48] C.R. Alford wrote:

> "The ceremony was performed by the *TGS*[49] *Trinidad*, and 'all Tobago and his wife' were there.

> "A line of flags was stretched between two beacons which mark the approach to the wharf from seaward. The *Trinidad* approached at dead slow speed and cut the flag line with her bow, blowing a salute from her siren as she did so. She then curved gracefully round and came gently alongside the wharf, where she blew a second salute. Captain Bodden …could not have handled his ship with more perfect skill."[50]

Four years later, January 31, 1957, the Harbour Master declared the *Trinidad* unseaworthy and pulled her out of service. Five days later, on February 4, the *Tobago* was withdrawn, ostensibly for repairs. The truth was that both vessels were in a parlous state. The 1957 Wharton Commission

---

[48] The Port of Spain deep water wharves went into operation in 1939.
[49] Trinidad Government Steamer.
[50] C.R Alford, *Island of Tobago,* p.21.

found that the only work done on the vessels for the first 16 years was the scraping and painting of their bottoms although the 1952 Cubitt survey (Lloyd's) had listed a number of repair problems that should have been addressed urgently.[51]

The Harbour Master gave the government no advance notice of his intention to pull the vessels out of service. Needless to say he gave the public no notice. Passengers were stranded. Trade came to a halt.

Tobago was again cut off from the world.

---

[51] Cubitt also said the *Trinidad* and *Tobago* had passed the stage where repairs could have prolonged their lives indefinitely.

CHAPTER VI

1957 - 1978

A parade of small vessels

The PNM government newly elected in September 1956 was not at all amused by the Harbour Master's decision. It immediately issued instructions to find replacements.

The Harbour Master's office hurriedly negotiated the charter of a number of small vessels:

- *Blue Star* (owned by Gaston Athanase of Martinique and Mr. Wallace from St.Vincent)

- *Silver* Arrow owned by Alston's

- *Zinnia*

- *William Johnston* (owned by a Trinidad businessman) and

- *t.b. Radar* [52] (owned by a Barbados businessman).

The *Zinnia* and the *t.b. Radar* came in time to save the 1957 Tobago Racehorse Spring Meeting. Over 60 horses were waiting to be shipped. Owners and race fans were anxious until the *Zinnia* arrived for its first sailing on February 8. She took some of the horses. The *t.b. Radar* left Port of Spain on her first trip on February 14 carrying 40 passengers, cargo and race horses. The charter cost $1,100 for each round trip between Trinidad and Tobago.

The chartered round-trip rate for the *m.v. Blue Star* was $1,250 with an additional $750 for the weekly trip around the Tobago coast.

The *m.v. Madinina*,[53] with a 174-passenger capacity, ran on weekends. She was chartered for 3 months, from June 1, to sail out of Port of Spain on Friday night and return from Scarborough on Monday morning. During the week the vessel went back to her regular operation between Trinidad and Grenada.

---

[52] The initials and surname of the original owner.

[53] Escala and Navarro of St. Vincent St., Port of Spain were the agents for the *Madinina*.

None of these vessels performed well. There were several breakdowns that left passengers stranded. The *Blue Star* ran aground in June; the *t.b. Radar* once remained at Scarborough for 6 days after limping into the harbour several hours after she was due to dock. The vessel had to be towed to Port of Spain.

The freighter *s.s. West India,* owned by the West Indian Navigation Co. Ltd., came to the rescue on three occasions in February and March.

The Harbour Master also chartered the *Caracas* for one day (February 5) to take cargo between Trinidad and Tobago since the schooners proved to be inadequate.

Amidst all this, travellers and shippers were complaining about the loss of cargo and pilfering.

The 1957 Wharton Commission of Inquiry

In March the Governor appointed a Commission of Inquiry chaired by the prominent barrister-at-law (attorney) Joseph Algernon Wharton to inquire into the breakdowns of the *Trinidad* and the *Tobago.*

In May the Commission submitted its report to the Governor who released it to the public at the end of that month. The report was a damning indictment of the government's neglect of the need for continuing maintenance of the vessels despite the several communications on the matter it had been receiving from the Harbour Master, the General Manager of the Port Services and A.P.T. James. That neglect clearly translated into indifference to the safety of passengers and crew.

The vessels had been withdrawn from the Lloyd's register in 1935 and not submitted to a survey until 1952 when the Lloyd's surveyor (J.C. Cubitt) declared that they were in "woeful condition."

The Commission noted that:

- A.P.T. James, member for Tobago, had tirelessly raised the condition of the vessels in the Legislative Council since 1947

- the Harbour Master and general manager of Port Services had submitted reports in 1943 and 1948 which called for refit and overhaul of the vessels

- in 1952 Lloyd's surveyor Cubitt had said the *Trinidad* would have to be taken out of service in 18 months and the *Tobago* in 2 years if major repairs were not carried out

- the search of the vessels' deck logs and other reports revealed overloads during August and at most weekends. On one occasion the *s.s Trinidad,* built for 120 passengers, carried 319 and; the *s.s Tobago,* built for 92, carried 403 passengers. "The captain's bridge and the engine room (on the *s.s Tobago*) were the only areas which were free of passengers."

The Commission found that:

- the *Trinidad* and the *Tobago* had been withdrawn from classification at Lloyd's in 1935 and no alternative standard had been adopted for the upkeep of the vessels

- the vessels were unseaworthy, obsolete and inadequate for passengers and goods traffic between the islands

- the government had been aware of the condition of the vessels since the 1940s through letters from the Harbour Master and the General Manager of Port Services and through the constant complaints that the Member for Tobago had been making both inside and outside the Legislative Council

- the government seemed not to be aware or to have lost sight of its role as a ship-owner whose duty was to practise a proper system of maintenance, not only to prolong the life of its vessels but also to ensure the safety of all who committed themselves or their property in good faith to its care

- the government's argument that it had first intended to replace the vessels after 15 years was unusual since the lives of properly maintained and managed vessels go way beyond 15 years

- in 1946 the government had decided to keep the vessels in service but had never withdrawn them for complete survey and repairs to be done at the same time

- the government was aware that the vessels were carrying passengers far beyond the authorised limits without due regard for the comfort and safety of the public [54] and

- successive Harbour Masters and General Managers of Port Services had been too ready to follow the apparent government policy relating to the ships and to their overcrowding without determining where it would lead.

So for 22 years, captain, crew and passengers travelled on vessels that were not insured contrary to international maritime law. The passengers, at least, were surely ignorant of the exposure.

---

[54] The 1938 report of the Nicholl Committee had brought the matter of the overcrowding of the *Trinidad* and the *Tobago* and passenger discomfort to the government's attention.

The Commission recommended that:

- the government should accept greater responsibility for securing a greater sense of discipline among its officers and the general public

- no funds should be invested in repair of the vessels

- the government should place the service in the hands of a competent and responsible authority (public or private) which would manage and control the ships and their crews

- vessels should at all times be maintained to the standards set by Lloyd's and similar societies.

The only bright spot in the Commission's report was its praise of the Captains and Chief Engineers and their crew. "In an otherwise unhappy picture," it said, "we consider that in circumstances that were sometimes difficult, the ships' Captains performed their duties creditably and the Engine Room Staff maintained a sense of responsibility that is reflected in the present condition of their department."

Sea communication between Trinidad and Tobago continued to be in a shambles.

1957 Steer inter-ministerial committee

Following the scathing report of the Wharton Commission the government looked for direction on the future of the coastal service. It appointed an inter-ministerial committee headed by government statistician H.J. Steer.[55]

The committee was to advise on the following scenarios:

- purchase of suitable ships and a government-operated service

- purchase of suitable ships and rental of them to private enterprise to operate the service under certain conditions

---

[55] Other members were: Lushington Bowen, acting Permanent Secretary, Ministry of Finance, Planning and Development; J. Superville, Permanent Secretary, Ministry of Works and Public Utilities; and Harbour Master, Captain J. Leal.

- private enterprise providing ships and
  operating the service under
  government direction.

The committee held its first meeting on July 11, 1957.

Just three days later, at 11 a.m. on Sunday, July 14, a vessel that would subsequently revolutionise travel between Tobago and Trinidad arrived in the Port of Spain harbour.

The *City of Port of Spain* – the first ferry

Built in 1948 along the lines of an invasion barge, the former *T.M.T. Cuba* was engaged in auto transport between Havana and Key West, Florida. Later re-converted for passenger and cargo service, it was re-christened the *City of Port of Spain.*

The *City of Port of Spain* caused an uproar on the docks. When she steamed into Port of Spain, docked and then dropped her stern ramp[56] to reveal her roll-on/roll-off capability, the jaws of stevedores and longshoremen dropped in unison. (We shall soon see why.)

---

[56] She also had a bow ramp.

Then the Martiniquan part-owner of the *Blue Star* swaggered into town claiming that the *City of Port of Spain* could carry 600 passengers and at the same time asserting ownership of the vessel. He offered to lease the vessel to the government. Members of the public were invited to tour the vessel; they were impressed.

With only one vessel on the route and passengers eager to travel, the Customs and Excise Department[57] issued a temporary licence for a trial run.

Almost 400 persons lined up for and purchased tickets. The government for its part lined up its special guests.

Stevedores and longshoremen also lined up to load the vessel. Normally, 2 gangs comprising 8 men each would load the inter-island vessels but the *City of Port of Spain* introduced palletised loading which cut the labour force by 50%. Four Ransomes (2 in the shed and 2 in the hold) and eight men loaded the vessel for its trial run.

On the morning of the trial run, Sunday, July 21, passengers and dignitaries arrived at the port of Port of Spain bright and early.

---

[57] All vessels involved in the 'Coasting Trade' must be licensed by the Customs and Excise Department. (see Chapter X).

But the government surveyor[58] had inspected the vessel and its certification including the Load Line Certificate[59] and ruled it was to carry no more than 300 persons inclusive of its 12-member crew. According to reports none of the government dignitaries were on board when the vessel sailed: 91 of the passengers with confirmed tickets, were also left behind.

On July 27 the government[60] announced that it would wet-lease the vessel provided the owner followed the recommendations of the government surveyor. The surveyor had called for the installation of separate toilet facilities for male and female deck passengers, an increase in the number of crew members from 12 to 30[61] to ensure passenger safety, etc.

But it was now almost time for the long Discovery holiday weekend[62] – a time of heavy passenger loads between Trinidad and Tobago. The government faced a major problem.

---

[58] The government surveyor was attached to the Ministry of Works and Transport.

[59] The Load Line Certificate is one of the most important documents on a vessel. It guides cargo volume and passenger load.

[60] Chief Minster, Dr. Eric Williams, was out of the country on official business.

[61] This was also done to have local staff employed on board the vessel. The practice continues.

[62] The 1st Monday in August was observed as Discovery Day, when Christopher Columbus was said to have "discovered" Trinidad. In fact, Columbus reached the island on July 31.

The *Madinina* was out of service. Trinidadians who were silent before were now raising their voices in protest over the poor service because they could not get to Tobago for their Discovery weekend.

The Customs Department then issued another temporary licence for the *City of Port of Spain* to make return trips over the weekend.

And then a company called T.M.T. Ferry Inc. got word to the government[63] that they were the legal owners of the *City of Port of Spain.*

Both parties were called in by the government which, only at this late stage, demanded to see a deed of ownership. Satisfied that T.M.T. Ferry Inc. was in fact the vessel's owner, the government signed an initial 3-month contract with the company on September 15, 1957. The *Blue Star's* part-owner did not contest the government's decision.

The contract, worth $3,400 per round trip, called for three round trips each week.

---

[63] Dr. Williams had by then returned to office.

City of Port of Spain Schedule

From P.O.S	From Scarborough
Monday 11 a.m.	Tuesday 11 a.m.
Wednesday 11 a.m.	Thursday 11 a.m.
Saturday[64] 1 p.m.	Sunday 12 midnight

To increase revenue the port stopped the 10% discount on return fares and opted to sell one-way tickets only. The single fare was $6.50 for tourist class and $3.00 for deck. (The classification of 2nd and 3rd class passengers had been changed to tourist and deck class).

With its roll on/roll off facility, the *City of Port of Spain* was the first ferry to travel between Trinidad and Tobago. That facility together with the 1953 opening of the wharf made for a faster turnaround of vessels at Scarborough.

Stevedores protested. Their jobs were being threatened.

---

[64] Government offices opened on Saturdays until 12 noon. Many public officers resident in Tobago travelled on this sailing to spend some time with their families.

At the time 75% of the staff employed with the inter-island vessels comprised stevedores, longshoremen and winchmen for the derricks. Some travelled from port to port and to the Tobago bays loading and offloading cargo. Two gangs of stevedores, each comprising 6 to 8 men, loaded cars on vessels. One gang worked on the wharf, placing each car in a net that was hoisted by the derricks fitted on the masts of the vessels. The other gang controlled the cars as they were lowered on the deck, untied the cars from the derricks and then strapped them down.[65]

With its roll on/roll off facility, the *City of Port of Spain* made all that work unnecessary.

But now, creatively, the port employed driver-stevedores.

The Radar and *The Caracas*

The *City of Port of Spain* was supplemented by the *t.b. Radar* which continued to suffer breakdowns. In October 1957, the government

---

[65] Before the Tobago wharf was opened in 1953, loading cars and cargo took much longer in Scarborough than it did in Port of Spain. Cars were first placed in nets, and then hoisted by cranes into lighters which then took the cars close to the vessels. From there the vehicles were raised by derricks onto the decks of the vessels for another gang of stevedores to deal with.

eventually chartered the *Caracas*, a small conventional freighter, to carry cargo between Port of Spain and Scarborough and to call at the bays in Tobago at a reported monthly cost of $14,000.

By this time the Tobago road system had developed to the stage where most of the cargo was shipped from and off-loaded at Scarborough. Proper roads were however yet to link the three villages of Bloody Bay, Parlatuvier and Castara to Scarborough.

The *Caracas* made 2 round trips per week and often carried deck passengers, presumably those who preferred to travel with their cargo.

Passenger single fare on the s.s. *Caracas:*

TO AND FROM PORT OF SPAIN	Deck
Bloody Bay	$2.50
Parlatuvier	$2.50
Castara	$2.50
Scarborough	$2.50

The Port Authority comes into being

The 1957 Steer Inter-ministerial Committee had recommended that:

- the coastal steamer service should be government-owned and operated

- two new vessels should be ordered for the service, and

- the Port Services should be separated from the Harbour Master's Office.

The government accepted the recommendations and in 1958 announced the separation of Port Services from the Harbour Master's Office. However, both agencies continued as Public Service bodies.

Three years later the name "Port Services" was changed to the "Port Authority of Trinidad and Tobago" (PATT) by the Port Authority Ordinance, No. 39 of 1961.

The 1961 Ordinance required PATT to run the Government Shipping Service (GSS) as a separate entity within the Authority and with separate accounts, personnel and berthing facilities.

In April 1980 PATT was transformed into a body corporate with continued responsibility for managing the GSS on behalf of the government.

The *Bird of Paradise* and the *Scarlet Ibis*

A Colonial Office note of March 3, 1959 states, "Agreement has been reached on the specifications of the two new steamers ordered for the Tobago service, and it is hoped that they will both be launched in 1959 and delivered in 1960."[66]

The specifications called for two vessels built along the lines of the *City of Port of Spain.* Christened the *m.v. Bird of Paradise* and the *m.v. Scarlet Ibis,* both vessels cost a total of $3,000,000.

Launched in November 1959, the *Bird of Paradise* arrived in Trinidad on February 16, 1960. The *Scarlet Ibis* came the following year. With a speed of 10½ knots, these motor vessels took 8-9 hours to go from port to port.

Captain Lorenzo Bodden was the first master of the *Bird of Paradise,*[67] which made its maiden

---

[66] Colonial Office reference CO 1031/2916.

[67] After Bodden retired Captain Eustace Urquhart, the first Master from Tobago, commanded the Bird of Paradise. Captains Bill Ellis, Eric Hall and Herman Ashton were the Masters of the Scarlet Ibis.

voyage to Tobago on February 23, 1960 with a number of specially invited guests.

There was much celebration at the Scarborough port. The Police Band entertained.

The Chief Minister Dr. Eric Williams toured the vessel as it swayed in the Scarborough harbour. Tobago schoolchildren enjoyed an hour-long demonstration voyage and snacks. The vessel returned to Trinidad in the early hours of the following day.

The *Bird of Paradise* and the *Scarlet Ibis* could each carry 300 passengers (100 tourist class and 200 in deck), 700 tons of cargo and 33 cars or 30 cars and one (1) truck. Because of the very low deck beams, the truck was the last vehicle to be loaded. The driver-stevedore had to reverse into the hold since the area just before the stern ramp was the only place where the front of a truck could fit.

The deck floors were made of teak. Every fortnight the crew scrubbed the floors with lye and sand and soap to remove grime and expose the beauty of the wood.

The vessels were also equipped with 100 wire cages in which vendors and other passengers secured their goods and baggage.

Each vessel made 4 return trips per week. They could not complete a return trip in 24 hours but they provided an almost daily service.

Passengers paid a single fare of $3.00 for deck, $6.50 for tourist class and $10.00 for cabins (there were only two (2) cabins). The port warned, however, that return cabin accommodation was not guaranteed.[68]

The schedule of sailings remained much the same as that of the *Trinidad* and the *Tobago*:

Day	*Bird of Paradise*	*Scarlet Ibis*
Sunday	No sailing. Docked in Port of Spain	Scarborough - PoS 10.00 p.m.
Monday	PoS - Scarborough 10.00 p.m.	Docked in Port of Spain
Tuesday	Scarborough - PoS 10.00 p.m.	PoS - Scarborough 10.00 p.m.
Wednesday	PoS - Scarborough 10.00 p.m.	Scarborough - PoS 10.00 p.m.
Thursday	Scarborough - PoS 10.00 p.m.	PoS - Scarborough 10.00 p.m.
Friday	PoS - Scarborough 10.00 p.m.	Scarborough - PoS 10.00 p.m.
Saturday	Scarborough - PoS 10.00 p.m.	PoS - Scarborough 12 noon

[68] Passenger fares issued by PATT for November 2 to December 1, 1970.

On Sundays, the only sailing was out of Scarborough and the vessels travelled from Scarborough on alternate weeks. But on long holiday weekends both vessels sailed on Sundays.

The *Scarlet Ibis* made fortnightly calls at the ports of Castara, Parlatuvier and Bloody Bay.

SCARLET IBIS
PORT OF SPAIN

Top Tobago public servant, Fitz Belle, (front) disembarks from the Scarlet Ibis at the end of her maiden voyage to Tobago.
Photo: courtesy Clement Williams.

Passengers on their way to Parlatuvier after disembarking from the Scarlet Ibis. At the time the road system did not link Parlatuvier to Scarborough.

Photos: Desmond Basso

In 1962, the *Bird of Paradise* and the *Scarlet Ibis* carried 108,466 passengers and 47,304 tons of cargo. The volume of traffic and cargo increased each year, leading the Port Authority to start barge shipment of cargo in 1968.

In October 1969, radar[69] was installed on the two vessels "to assist Masters and Officers in navigation regardless of weather conditions and to ensure the safety of passengers and crew."[70]

Confident with their new navigation aids, the vessels made excursion trips to Grenada and Venezuela and in the Gulf of Paria in 1970.

The boats were regularly serviced and were surveyed every four years according to standards set by Lloyds. Overcrowding on weekends and long holidays continued.

The Annual Report of the Port Authority for 1972 stated, "The Tobago Shipping Service was hard pressed and thought should be given to obtaining a cargo boat for this service."

One year later (1973), the Port Authority urged "after 13 years of service... it is not too early to start thinking of replacing these ships *(Scarlet Ibis* and *Bird of Paradise)*."

---

[69] Up to this time, Masters and Officers navigated by sight.
[70] Annual Report of the Port Authority 1969.

The *m.v. Tobago* arrives, fails and leaves

Passenger and freight demand caused the government to start looking for new vessels.

The government attempted to source vessels through government-to-government arrangements but found that there were no government-owned ferry services in the European countries they approached.

They were then persuaded to send a team to Venezuela to negotiate for a vessel. This approach led to much public debate as people questioned the ability of the negotiating team even to understand Spanish, let alone speak it.[71]

The government settled on the *m.v. Santa Margarita* which was built in 1970 by a Dutch company to run between Margarita and mainland Venezuela[72] and purchased the vessel in August 1976 for $10.2m and re-named it the *m.v. Tobago*. She arrived in late August with a captain, chief

---

[71] In a letter published in the *Daily Express* of July 10, 1981, Carlton A. Goddard of Belmont, a former marine engineer at the port and a member of the negotiating team, said that negotiations for the *m.v. Tobago* were conducted in English and that the Trinidad and Tobago government ignored the recommendations of the technocrats on the unsuitability of the vessel.

[72] During the voyage from Pampata (Margarita) to Punto la Cruz (Venezuela), the vessel had to traverse the Bora – an area of turbulent and treacherous water. The vessel was hardy enough to cross the Bocas.

engineer and a motor man (oiler) on a 3-month contract.

Like the *City of Port of Spain,* the vessel had both bow and stern ramps but the bow ramp was never used. The deck beams on the *m.v. Tobago* were so high that on its demonstration run on Saturday, September 4, a soft drink production machine was loaded to the cheers of workers. The workers had watched the machine languishing on the wharf for months, waiting to be barged to Tobago.

Vendors travelled for free. Tobago students who went to school in Trinidad were offered free tickets for the return trip (the new school year was to start the following Monday). There also was a long list of dignitaries.[73] These gestures led to agitation by the opposition, in and from Tobago, which accused the government of using the vessel for election purposes.[74]

Meanwhile, the government surveyor had found shortcomings in the vessel. There was no dining room for officers and the vessel did not offer them adequate cabin accommodation. Further, the surveyor pointed out, the Master of the vessel would

---

[73] Very few paying passengers were on board. At that time September was a slack month for travel from Port of Spain.

[74] General elections were to be held later that month (September).

have to share toilet and bath facilities with his crew (a situation that is unheard of on any respectable vessel).

The surveyor ruled that the shortcomings were to be corrected before the vessel could be put into regular service.

The government then invited tenders to build a dining room for officers, to provide adequate cabin accommodation for officers, and to construct toilet and bath facilities for the Master. The work was swiftly completed and the *m.v. Tobago* went into regular service in October with a local captain because soon after the demonstration trip, and long before the 3-month contract had expired, the Venezuelan captain and motorman (oiler) left the vessel to return to Venezuela.[75] Local Captain Eric (Jimmy) Hall became the Master of the vessel.

The *m.v. Tobago* ran on the following daylight schedule:

Departs Port of Spain	Arrives Scarborough	Departs Scarborough	Arrives Port of Spain
6 a.m.	Between 11.30 a.m. and 12 noon	2 p.m.	7.30 p.m.

[75] Interview and discussions with Desmond Basso, Chief Engineer, May - September 2005.

This schedule was clearly inappropriate for traffickers, business and other users. They had to rely on the *Bird of Paradise* which had maintained her night schedule while the *Scarlet Ibis* worked between Claxton Bay and Scarborough - the cement run.

The *m.v. Tobago* sailed on but there was constant activity in the engine room where malfunctioning of the equipment prevailed.

The Venezuelan chief engineer appeared to be overwhelmed by the number of engine problems. One evening he simply left the vessel. He was last seen boarding a fishing boat at the open wharves or Caricom jetty.[76]

It was left to local chief engineer, Desmond Basso, to assume leadership, but he was confronted with manuals and documents written in Spanish and Dutch, not to mention equipment so labelled.

Nevertheless, he and his crew had the ship ready to sail out at 6 o'clock the next morning.

At his own expense, Basso had some of the manuals translated into English and with his crew explored the engine room to discover where pipelines began and ended.

---

[76] Basso interview.

There were major engine and gearbox problems.

On January 28, 1977, after 3 months on the route, one engine failed close to Chaguaramas, on the way to Tobago. It was possible to complete the journey on one engine but the crankshaft on the starboard engine failed on the north coast. The vessel could go no further. The PATT tugboat, *Snapper,* had to tow the vessel with 170 passengers on board back to Port of Spain.

The then Chairman of the Port Authority, Eustace Bernard, cried: "I have not ruled out the possibility of sabotage."

Happily, the *Scarlet Ibis* was relieved of cargo duty to join the *Bird of Paradise* on the passenger run. Both vessels continued to perform admirably. But a larger vessel was needed.

The 1957 Gregoire Commission of Inquiry

As for the *m.v. Tobago,* the government appointed a Commission of Inquiry in late March 1977 to inquire into "all the circumstances, including the negotiations, surrounding and leading to the acquisition of the vessel."

The Commission, headed by the Auditor General, Errol Gregoire, heard evidence from several port officials.

The breakdown of the vessel was discussed and Bernard aired his sabotage theory. Francis Mungroo, the Secretary General of the Seamen and Waterfront Workers' Trade Union (SWWTU), was incensed. In his evidence, he outlined the sequence of events that had led to the breakdown and eventual towing of the *m.v.Tobago*. There was no sabotage, he said. The vessel simply could not sail.

Captain Eric Hall told the Commission that he was instructed by his seniors not to run the vessel at full speed and that they suggested he stay below three-quarter speed at all times.

Chief Engineer Basso related that the port engine failed because the Dressler coupling that joined the oil pipes had slipped out - oil was being pumped into the bilge. The engine was therefore running without an oil supply. Basso explained that the vessel had no alarm system to alert engineers that lubricating oil was not reaching the port engine. In addition, he said, the coupling and oil pipes were located under the floor plate of the engine room.

Joseph Pounder, Commissioner of the Board of Inland Revenue and a member of the Commission, said "the importance of this situation was that all the log books of that vessel were written in Spanish."

However, the Commission's report called on the government "to give immediate consideration to the vessel's readiness, putting it into a state of repair, and to obtaining appropriate spare parts for the future operation of the vessel."

The Commission argued that the cost of repairing the *m.v. Tobago* would be far less than what would be needed for a new vessel.

But the vessel continued to rock useless and listless alongside the jetty for a little over four years. In February 1981, she left Port of Spain, under tow, for Holland where her manufacturer was to do a refit.

CHAPTER VII

1979 - 1984

Almost three years after the breakdown of the *m.v. Tobago,* opposition member A.N.R. Robinson moved a motion in the House of Representatives in November 1979 calling on the government to appoint a Commission of Enquiry into the use of the *m.v. Tobago* for election purposes. The motion was passed unanimously.

In June 1980 the government announced in the House of Representatives the appointment of a one-man Commission to investigate the operation and use of the *m.v. Tobago* in the 1976 election. The Commissioner was Richard Toby, who had among his terms of reference "to make recommendations including any draft legislation that may be deemed necessary to prevent public funds from being used for party electioneering and to guarantee free and fair elections in the future…"

The Commission held its first meeting on October 19, 1980. Its report exonerated the government.

The 1979 Ryan Commission of Inquiry

The Ryan Commission of Inquiry was appointed by His Excellency the President, Sir Ellis Clarke, on December 7, 1979 to enquire into –

"All aspects of Port operations in Trinidad and Tobago and in particular to enquire into:

a. the problem of congestion on the ports;

b. the system of overtime employment on the ports;

c. the effect that such overtime employment has on the levels of employment in the country;

d. the salaries, wages, allowances and other terms and conditions of service of employees engaged at the ports;

e. the resultant costs to the consumer of goods and other commodities passing through the ports;

f. the availability of and the type of equipment used on the ports, taking into account acceptable standards of safety;

g. matters incidental thereto."

By instrument dated 25 February, 1980 the President altered the terms of reference to include inquiry into:

> "the question of overtime payment to supervisory personnel employed by the Port Authority."

The Commission, chaired by Dr. Selwyn Ryan, comprised in addition Richard Toby, Herman Marcano and Ina Nicholson, Marine Adviser to the government.

The Government Shipping Service (GSS) was naturally part of the Commission's mandate. Hearings covered cargo shipping, which the Commission found to be grossly inadequate.

Passenger and warehousing facilities were deemed to be unacceptable, as were the supply and maintenance of equipment at both Port of Spain and Scarborough. The Commission was also told that forklifts or equipment sent from Scarborough to Trinidad for repairs were seldom returned expeditiously, but were kept in Port of Spain to alleviate shortages being experienced there.

In its report the Commission expressed alarm over the reports of pilferage and losses. It said:

> "The business community has reported that claims valued at millions of dollars have been lodged against the Port Authority. Many of them have not been honoured by the Authority.
>
> "...(T)he Boat Note provides that 'no claim for any package of any description whatsoever will be admitted beyond the value of three dollars unless such excess value be declared at the time of shipment and insurance paid thereon at the rate of five per cent on such declared value'."

The Commission pointed out, however, that many users of the service were not in the habit of purchasing insurance coverage. It went on to say that the Port Authority itself made no attempt to verify that cargo entered on the Boat Note was in fact received and that the Authority might well have honoured claims for cargo that it had never received. To correct this deficiency, the Commission recommended the Port Authority should *inter alia:*

> "ensure that cargo entered on the Boat is *in fact received.* As it is now, the Port Authority makes no attempt to verify this and may well be paying claims for cargo that it never received. The receiving clerk should be closely supervised."

The Commission went on to say that:
> "badly secured cargo should be refused for shipping
>
> all goods should be tallied on to the ship by the ship's clerk who should be responsible to the Captain
>
> cargo should be tallied off the ship by the Ship's Clerk and a receiving Clerk

high-value goods should be shipped
in properly secured containers

high-value goods should be kept in
a secured area with two (2) locks
to be opened and closed by two (2)
senior officers who should each
have a key to a lock. No one officer
should have the keys to both locks.
An inventory of high-value goods
should be kept

the hold should be locked by the
Ship's Clerk who should be on
board to deliver the cargo at the
opposite end

delivery of cargo should be closely
supervised."

The Ryan Report meshed with the findings of
the Richardson Andrews team which had examined
shipping within and between Caricom countries in
late 1977.

The 1977 Andrews Report lamented the
absence of safety equipment on board the vessels
(mainly schooners) that transported passengers
and cargo, the use of unqualified sailors and the

absence of First Aid and other medical supplies, and the absence of life jackets and life boats. The Report also called for the early installation of communication devices on the vessels.

On the ferry service between Trinidad and Tobago the Andrews Report pointed to:

- inefficient and poor handling of cargo

- poor scheduling of vessels, and

- inadequate management of the service.

Meanwhile, the government had been actively searching for a vessel. Offers came from mainly European ship owners and the government had dispatched technical teams to inspect the vessels on offer.[77] The technocrats advised the government to turn down the offers. Then in 1980, a technical team came across a vessel it thought ideal for the ferry service.

---

[77] Richardson Andrews headed one of these teams which comprised the Port marine engineer and Ina Nicholson. The owner of a vessel in southern France had offered his ship to the government. The Andrews team visited southern France to examine the vessel and Andrews recalls that the owner refused to show them the plans for the vessel. The team naturally advised the government not to engage in further discussions on purchase of that vessel.

The ports of Port of Spain and Scarborough got new life. There was activity on land and sea. The Government Shipping Service (GSS) berth in Port of Spain was completed and the GSS office renovated to accommodate the increasing passenger load. In Tobago there was feverish dredging of the harbour. By early October, both ports were ready to welcome the vessel that was to become the benchmark for reliability and punctuality.

The *m.f. Gelting*

On October 15, 1980, the *m.f. Gelting* arrived from Denmark on a 2-year charter at the rate of $16,800 a day.[78]

Charter of the vessel was negotiated by the Chairman of the Port Authority, the Port Marine Engineer, and Ina Nicholson.

The *Gelting,* with 15 cabins and capacity for 1,000 passengers, 125 cars and cargo, remains the standard by which the ferry service is judged. Passengers of the 1980s recall her on-time arrivals and departures and the fact that she ran without incident for the 7 years of her stay in this country.

---

[78] The return fares on the Gelting were: cabin - $20.00, tourist class - $13.00.

She made her maiden voyage to Tobago on October 25, 1980.

One clause of the charter contract called for the vessel to make daily return trips.

The *Bird of Paradise* was to run alongside the *Gelting* taking passengers and cargo from Port of Spain at night while the *Scarlet Ibis* returned to the transport of cement from Claxton Bay to Scarborough.

The port then designed the following schedule:

Gelting Schedule

DAY	Port of Spain	Scarborough
Monday - Thursday	Arrives 5 a.m. Departs 12 noon	Arrives 7 p.m. Departs 11 p.m.
Friday	Arrives 5 a.m. Departs 5 p.m.	Arrives 12 noon Departs 11.59 p.m.
Saturday	Arrives 6 a.m. Departs 12 noon.	Arrives 7 p.m.
Sunday	No sailing	Departs 10.00 p.m.

Everyone complained about the inconvenience of that schedule where the boat arrived in Trinidad at 5 a.m. and left at 12 noon,[79] giving no time to transact business. It was impossible for Tobago traffickers to buy and sell produce at the PoS market and get back to the port for the return trip. Truckers complained that the schedule was impeding their business.[80] They had to stay in Trinidad for an additional day and time was money.

Then, to the astonishment of regular users, the port authorities placed the *Gelting* on "Special Sailings" to transport race horses and to facilitate holiday makers and race fans who wished to visit Tobago for the Divali [81] holiday and for the Tobago *Flamboyant Races* in November 1980.

The "Special Sailings" were in effect from Thursday, November 6 to Sunday, November 9. According to the schedule, the vessel left Trinidad on the Thursday, Saturday and Sunday at 10 p.m., 6 a.m. and 5 a.m. respectively. On Monday, November 10 the port reverted to its 12 noon departure from Port of Spain.

---

[79] Regular users of the service felt they were being denied the comfort of the boat.

[80] The construction sector in Tobago was booming.

[81] Divali was observed on Friday, November 7 that year and the races were held on November 8.

After months of constant complaints the port management settled for a 2 p.m. Port of Spain departure which went into effect on June 6, 1981. The Tobago departure was then fixed at 11 p.m. The *Gelting* therefore became the first vessel to complete a daily return voyage between Trinidad and Tobago, with a schedule that fitted the needs of the regular clients.[82] The vessel did not sail on Saturdays except at peak periods.[83]

The height of the deck beams on the vessel coupled with the size of the hold also made it possible for the port to begin rental of large containers.

The travelling public was contented until Port Authority Chairman Bernard decreed in early July 1981 that vehicles had to remain on board until 7 a.m., the start of the working day on the port.

Business interests, drivers and passengers protested because the *Gelting* arrived in Port of Spain at 4.30 a.m. What was this extraordinary delay about? What had led Chairman Bernard to issue this edict?

He had discovered that workers assigned to help manage the safe disembarkation of vehicles and passengers received a "deprivation" (of sleep)

---

[82] The *Panorama* and the *Beauport* maintained the schedule.

[83] On Saturdays the vessel remained in Port of Spain for routine maintenance.

allowance for the early morning duty. A handful turned up for work while the majority slept at home (or elsewhere) and later collected their allowance.

Bernard gave orders to stop the allowance and declared that no one was to report for duty before normal working hours. He placed locked barricades on the quayside to prevent drivers from moving off the vessel until the workers reported for duty at 7 a.m. The travelling public was livid.

But another industrial matter had already been brewing. The stevedores wanted to have re-instated the practice of driving passengers' vehicles on and off the ferry. From the early days of vehicle transport between Trinidad and Tobago, drivers had to hand over their car keys to a clerk stationed at the cargo entrance of the embarkation port. The port's driver-stevedores would then take vehicles to the wharf for loading. At the disembarkation port the driver-stevedore would take vehicles from the vessel to the wharf, then hand the keys to the clerk who would in turn hand them over to the drivers.

This ceremony continued with the *Scarlet Ibis* and the *Bird of Paradise* which arrived in Port of Spain at 4.30 a.m. According to the terms of engagement, the clerk was the middleman between driver-stevedores and vehicle owners or drivers, so it was not until 7 a.m. when port staff reported for duty that the ceremony could begin. Owners or drivers were expected to collect their keys at the cargo gate from 8 a.m. And one could not of course expect the hand-over ceremony to take place during lunch hours.

Chairman Bernard would have none of this driver-stevedore-handing-over-of-keys business. He declared that passengers were quite capable of driving on and off the *Gelting,* as was the practice with ferries all over the world.

The workers agitated – they were being deprived of their "deprivation" allowance and being told that there was no need for their driving skills.

The port management and the SWWTU finally reached an agreement in which a supervisor and four workers were to report for the vessel's arrival at 4.30 a.m.; the workers were to receive overtime payment and some driver-stevedores were retained to "choc" vehicles so they remained steady on the voyage between the islands and to 'un-choc' them at the end of the voyage.[84]

Drivers were now to take their vehicles on board where they were "choced" and to drive off the vessel when the port workers "unchoced" at the end of the voyage. Everyone was contented.

---

[84] This practice still continues.

Meanwhile, the high petroleum export prices that the country had been earning in the late 1970s had dropped sharply but wild spending in Trinidad and Tobago continued. Cargo space on the ferry service was at a premium and in 1983 the government leased the cargo vessel *Teisten* to run alongside the *Gelting*.

The *Bird of Paradise* then joined the *Scarlet Ibis* in the transport of cement from Claxton Bay.

The *Gelting* went off the Trinidad-Tobago route in 1987 and was bought by Conferry, a Margarita interest, which re-named her the *Santa Rita*.

The *m.v. Tobago* returns and runs aground

On August 18, 1981 a repaired *m.v. Tobago* re-entered the country with two new engines fitted in Holland and with a Dutch captain and chief engineer on a one-year contract. Also on board the vessel were Captain Herman Ashton, Chief Engineer David Daniel[85] and sixty 20 ft.-containers[86] which Chairman Bernard and his technical team had bought in France.

---

[85] Bernard had flown to Holland to inspect the vessel, with his technical team. They also went to France to buy containers. Tobago businessmen had earlier started to build "containers" for their goods in an attempt to deter pilfering.

[86] The containers which are still in use and painted in green, are identified by numbers, e.g., 1/60

The refit of the vessel had a cost of $8 million.

It was time for a trial run between Trinidad and Tobago. The refurbished vessel sailed out on August 21 and on that trial run the local marine engineers discovered a defective part in the gearbox of the port main engine.

With the memory of the original purchase of the vessel and its subsequent difficulties still fresh, the port officials refused to take delivery of the *m.v. Tobago* until the contractors had corrected the problem. Only when satisfied did the port experts accept the vessel[87] and put it in service alongside the *Gelting* from August 23.

The contract of the Dutch captain and chief engineer ended in mid-August 1982, and Captain Ashton and Chief Engineer Daniel took over. One month later, in the early morning of September 14, the *m.v.Tobago* ran aground in Dipdell (Lowlands), not far from the Scarborough port.

The night before, the Master (Captain Ashton) had safely guided the vessel out of the Port of Spain harbour and the Bocas. He handed over to his 3rd Mate, who in turn later handed over to the 2nd Mate

---

[87] The new engines were much too powerful for the gearboxes which had not been changed. Parts had to be purchased so frequently that the port authorities eventually bought new gearboxes.

for the penultimate leg of the trip. The Master was to return to the bridge when the "leading lights" of Scarborough came into view. He would then guide the vessel past the menacing Bulldog Reef (which has the reputation of being able to pass through the hull of a vessel like knife through butter) and into the Scarborough port.[88]

Everything seemed to be going smoothly when there was suddenly a violent impact. The Master rushed out of his cabin only to be embraced by coconut trees and branches. 82 passengers were jolted out of their sleep. The vessel had run aground.

Passengers were airlifted by helicopter. Later in the day the vessel was pulled out by a PATT tug but was able to proceed on her own to Scarborough to discharge cargo. She then returned to Port of Spain where she was greeted by the police led by the late Commissioner Randolph Burroughs.

The Chairman of the Port Authority, still holding fast to his previous sabotage theory, had called in the police. Nonsense, the SWWTU replied, the Master and crew would never place their lives and those of their passengers at risk.

---

[88] A ship bringing sand to Tobago from Guyana a few years ago is believed to have had its hull punctured by a reef. The vessel and her crew disappeared somewhere between Scarborough and Crown Point.

Meanwhile, Tobago groaned.

An enquiry was held in Tobago. At the end the Master (the person who has ultimate responsibility for safety and security on his vessel) was re-assigned to the *Scarlet Ibis*. He carried cement to Tobago for about 3-4 years before he retired from the port.

The 2nd Mate was re-assigned to a barge moving mud dredged from the Port of Spain harbour – unglamorous but useful work because the port needed to dredge the harbour to accommodate vessels with longer drafts.

The enquiry also exposed the port's promotion practices and its approach to certification of its seamen and officers.[89]

---

[89] The Ryan Commission also considered the matter of crew training and certification. In its report the Commission said that it was "...of the opinion that steps should be taken to have a proper training programme in maritime studies instituted so as to ensure an adequate source of seamen to crew vessels of the coastal service."

In 1987 PATT commissioned Captain Lalor of Jamaica to report on the operations of the Marine Department. Lalor found that two-thirds of the officers' positions were filled by unqualified persons.

The *m.v. Tobago* goes back into service

The *m.v. Tobago* was tough. The steel hull was only slightly damaged when she ran aground but it took about a year to have the repairs done. She went back in service.

It was at this time that a major change was made. Officers on the inter-island ferry got a new work schedule. They were to be on duty for two weeks followed by two weeks off. This was a drastic change in the work culture where officers and crew were attached to the vessels for over one year, sometimes two years, with no time off except for vacation and sick leave and occasional days.[90] The crew however continued to be attached to the vessels for long periods.

The *m.v. Tobago's* colourful history is not all about mishaps. After she returned to the sea bridge, she performed magnificently alongside the *m.v. Gelting* and then the *m.f. Panorama,* although her gearboxes regularly needed repairs. With her high deck beam she was the first ferry that could

---

[90] It is believed that quite a few of those who worked on the ferry service had families in both Trinidad and Tobago. Families and relationships were shattered or damaged because of the long absences of the men who were ferrying passengers and cargo between the two islands. Some wives felt that their husbands were married to the vessels. There were, however, many strong families that survived.

accommodate trucks. She carried 60 cars and 600 passengers. With a speed of 18-20 knots she went from port to port in five to six hours.

The *Bird of Paradise* and the *Scarlet Ibis* are retired

With the *Gelting, Teisten* and *m.v. Tobago* in service, the *Bird of Paradise* and the *Scarlet Ibis* were retired. They remained tied up on the docks until a small group of young Trinidad and Tobago entrepreneurs bought the *Bird of Paradise* and renamed her the *Maverick.*

The *Maverick* made a few trips to other Caribbean islands and to Guyana but the owners defaulted on their loan and the bank seized her. She was sold to a dive enthusiast who wanted to develop a dive site for novice divers. In 1997 he contracted a dive shop in Tobago to sink the ship in 100 feet of water at Mt. Irvine Bay.

The *Scarlet Ibis* remained tied up in the Port of Spain harbour at the Caricom wharf for years, slowly taking in water, slowly sinking, until she had collected enough water to disappear into the sea.

The *m.v. Tobago* is retired

By the mid 1990s the *m.v. Tobago* was considered outdated and slow. She ended her ferry run carrying mainly cargo before she was pulled out of service and eventually sold to a Caribbean shipping magnate from St. Vincent in February 2001. The Port Authority had invited tenders for her sale. All the interested parties offered prices way below what the Authority considered reasonable. The bidders argued that the vessel was only fit for scrap, but the eventual purchaser made an offer that was above the Authority's upset price. The purchaser is at present refitting the vessel for cargo and passenger runs among Caricom states.

Plotting a trade route

In late 1977 the cargo ship *Mercedes,* owned by Navarro's, struck a reef on its way into the Scarborough port. Quick action by the captain and crew of the *Scarlet Ibis* saved the *Mercedes* which had started sinking under the weight of its cargo as water poured into the vessel through large holes where the reef had caused damage.

The Port Authority sought to avert such an accident on the inter-island ferry and asked

Captain Ashton, Master of the *Scarlet Ibis*, to map out a trade route for navigation charting between Port of Spain and Scarborough.

Ashton presented the trade route on February 14, 1978. It was endorsed by Masters Eustace Urquhart, Edgar Johnston and Eric Hall. Hall was at this time acting as Marine Superintendent.

The Masters' enthusiasm over the introduction of the charting of a trade route was not shared by their crew who felt comfortable with the old method of navigating by sight. It would take 2½ years before navigational charting was introduced on the ferry service. The Master of the *Gelting* requested the trade route before he took the vessel out on her maiden voyage in October 1980. Captain Ashton was his pilot.

Desmond Basso recorded these stages of the Scarborough port.

CHAPTER VIII

1985 - 2000

The *m.f. Panorama*

In July 1985 the Trinidad and Tobago Gazette gave notice that government was inviting tenders for the design and construction of a new vessel specifically built for the ferry run and to be delivered in July 1987.[91]

A German firm[92] won the tender and the government with advice from technocrats settled on a vessel designed in part like the *Gelting*.

The 116-million dollar *mf Panorama* arrived

---

[91] While they were waiting on the new vessel the port introduced colour-coded tickets in September 1986 and ended the sale of return tickets. This was one of the many attempts to deal with the vexed question of overbooking and overloading of vessels.

[92] The company went out of business after the vessel was delivered. Many other builders had closed down because new ship-building technology was required for the construction of containerised cargo vessels. Germany is now among the world leaders in building these vessels.

on December 3, 1987[93] with a German crew and three local captains. Captains Alexis (then acting as Assistant Harbour Master), Lloyd de Roche and Edward Duncan had gone to Germany to meet the vessel and to familiarise themselves with its operations because local officers were to take full control at the end of the 3-week delivery contract with the builders.

The *Panorama* was launched as the first vessel to be registered in Trinidad and Tobago (Registration no. TT001)[94] under the recently proclaimed Shipping Act 1987, which provided for the registration of vessels in Trinidad and Tobago.

One year earlier (December 1986) there had been a change in government but the newly-elected government (NAR) closely followed the script of its predecessor – it was as if the protests of September 1976 over the *m.v. Tobago* had not happened. When the *Panorama* made its maiden voyage to Tobago on December 10, 1987, a long line of government dignitaries and invitees sailed out for Scarborough at 9 a.m. There was great festivity on board.

The Scarborough harbour had already been dredged and the pier extended for the new ferry.[95]

---

[93] Five (5) months after the gazetted delivery date.

[94] The *m.v. Tobago* carried Registration no. TT002.

[95] The deep-water harbour was completed in May 1991.

118

In Scarborough, the Prime Minister, A.N.R. Robinson, addressed the gathering. He said that the vessel was not only a link between Trinidad and Tobago but it was the country's link to the international community. The members and coach of the Signal Hill Comprehensive School football team were special guests at the event. They were lauded for their successes in that year's football season. The public was also invited to tour the vessel. There was great excitement in Scarborough.

The *Panorama* returned to Port of Spain the following day (December 11) short of several ashtrays and some of the lighting and plumbing fixtures. The pilfering never stopped.

In Port of Spain there were two days of public tours.

The vessel was about to go into regular service when it was discovered that local Captains employed on the port were all holders of the Master Home Trade Certificates only.[96] However, the tonnage

---

[96] In a 1937 despatch, the British Board of Trade sought information on the qualifications of all local officers who worked on the coastal steamer service. The Governor advised them that all local officers held Jamaican Home Trade Certificates. The Jamaica training institute was established by the colonial government to train marine officers from its colonies in the West Indies. Now Trinidad and Tobago nationals either go to Jamaica for training or follow a training programme of the Marine Division so that they can qualify to be officers on the inter-island ferry. Foreign Trade Certificates are pursued in the developed countries.

of the *Panorama*, 5300 tons, required officers with international experience and certification.

The government quickly signed a one-year contract with the captain and officers of the *Gelting*.[97]

The *m.f. Panorama* was outfitted with hanging car decks. It contained 25 double passenger cabins below the main deck and had capacity for 140 cars[98] and 650 passengers; special cabins for vendors; toilet facilities for the physically challenged and a conference room (the Scarlet Ibis Room[99]) with up-to-date facilities. However, the availability of the conference facilities was never advertised and so the vessel earned no revenue from the space.

The passenger cabins were located below deck. The design followed that of the *Gelting* which was not a passenger ship but a vessel for transporting trucks and itinerant workers between European ports. The truckers shared communal baths. On the Panorama it was cabin passengers who had to share these facilities.

---

[97] The *Gelting* charter had come to an end.

[98] One (1) truck with a tray takes up the space utilised by three (3) cars.

[99] The main cafeteria was located in the Cocrico Room and the smaller cafeteria in the Bird of Paradise Room.

This was a major flaw in the *Panorama's* design. The location of the cabins – under the car deck and at the bottom of the vessel – might have made the cabin passengers vulnerable had there been a disaster on board.

On the positive side, the height of her deck beams made it possible for higher vehicles and containers to be shipped between the islands.

Just as the government was contemplating renewing the contract with the *Gelting* officers, Captain Herman Ashton, now retired, returned to Trinidad and Tobago from working on vessels abroad. He happened to hear a news item in which the Minister responsible for the port stated that there was no local person capable and certified to command the *m.f. Panorama.*

Captain Ashton immediately gathered up his International Trade Certificate and other documents and headed to the port to meet with Ferdie Ferreira, Deputy General Manager of the Port Authority. Ferreira checked the documents, found them valid and immediately called the Minister to let him know that he was going to pay him a visit, accompanied by a certified local captain.

In five days Captain Ashton was on the bridge of the *m.f. Panorama* giving the necessary orders for the vessel to sail out of Port of Spain. He was the Master, and he stayed with the vessel for 14 years except for a brief period as the Pilot on the *Beauport.*[100]

Captain Alfred Mc Millan was later transferred from the *m.v. Tobago* to the *Panorama* and the Master's roster of two weeks on and two weeks off went into effect.

Like the *m.v. Tobago* and *m.f. Gelting,* the *Panorama* had speeds of 18-20 knots. But it was a bigger vessel with a weight of 5300 tons.

The *Panorama* was built as a ferry and for long runs. This has caused some problems, because given the short distance between Trinidad and Tobago, she has no time to run on "intermediate fuel" for fuel efficiency. (This she does on excursion trips to other Caribbean islands.)

Also on board the *Panorama* were cadets[101] in training to become deck and engine officers. Two of them were Nicole Quashie and Kimraj Gangaram, who later successfully completed the local and international examinations and became Masters of the *Panorama*. Quashie was the first female Captain on the ferry service.

---

[100] Masters on the ferry service perform pilot duty on wetlease vessels until their Masters become familiar with the route.

[101] The Port Authority started a Cadet programme in which young persons were trained to be deck and engine room officers.

Wasim Mohammed as a cadet officer in 1999. Wasim will complete International Chief Mate Certification in 2007.

Photo: Clarence Clarke.

The public is unhappy again

One would have thought that after 60 years of a government shipping service the GSS would have a clear user profile and could schedule the *m.f. Panorama* and the *m.v. Tobago* to suit the needs of its clients. The protest over the timing of the initial runs of the *Gelting* was recent enough to have been instructive. Yet the port management first scheduled the *Panorama* to leave Port of Spain at 7 a.m. After passenger protest they decided on the following schedule for the vessels:

Vessel	Departs POS	Arrives[102] Scarborough	Departs Scarborough	Arrives POS
Panorama	9 a.m.	1.30 p.m.	5 p.m.	10 p.m.
m.v. Tobago	2.30 p.m.	8 p.m.	11.30 p.m.	4 a.m.

The new and larger *Panorama* that could carry large containerised cargo and large trucks was therefore scheduled to operate at inconvenient times while the *m.v. Tobago* ran in the ideal time slot.

---

[102] Arrival times are not usually printed on the schedule because sailing conditions, for example, determine arrivals.

Passengers and business interests had to protest once again. The sailing schedule was changed to a *Panorama* departure at 2 p.m. from Port of Spain with an 11 p.m. departure from Scarborough. The *m.v. Tobago* left Port of Spain at 11 p.m.

By the early 1990s, passengers, traffickers and business persons were grumbling once again. The service was becoming progressively worse.

At peak times for local tourism - Easter, Christmas, long holiday weekends and the August holidays - the *m.f. Panorama* would be taken out of service for repairs and dry docking.[103] The *m.v. Tobago* would be left to service the run alone even though the pattern of travel showed that at least two vessels were needed at all times for the ferry service to be efficient.

The *m.v. Tobago* was far too small. Tickets were sold out very quickly. Businesses were being affected; vendors could not trade with confidence; truckers were up in arms since they were never certain when their vehicles would be leaving the

---

[103] Annual Reports of the Port Authority in the 1970s indicate that annual dry-docking and the compulsory four-year survey of the *Scarlet Ibis* and the *Bird of Paradise* took place during April and June. "Because of the exigencies of the service which demanded an almost daily shuttle between Trinidad and Tobago, there were no long lay-off periods." Dry-docking was done in the "low season". But since the mid-1990s there has been continuous high passenger and cargo demand.

port; the hospitality industry was crying foul; and consumer prices in Tobago, already significantly higher than those in Trinidad, were rising.

In addition, when the *m.f. Panorama* was not on dry dock it would at times be tied up awaiting parts which had either not been ordered in time or had not been ordered at all. There were also credit problems.[104]

The port management explained to the government (PNM) that the ferry service was operating a huge deficit and proposed in January 1993 that the one-way fare be increased to $50.00. The government promptly turned down the proposal.[105] The port had proffered the same argument to the NAR government when it sought a fare increase in 1989. That government, like its successor, had given short shrift to the argument.

---

[104] For two weeks in October 1993, the *Panorama* waited to go on dry dock because the port suppliers had refused to grant further credit. In November 2000, the *Panorama* waited for 6 days before a damaged propeller was repaired.

Masters of the vessels have complained that although they are responsible for carrying thousands of passengers between the islands their requests to meet with top management are often ignored and that their requisitions for spare parts are pronounced on by persons who are unfamiliar with the nature of the service.

[105] In 1998 the government increased the return fare to $50.00. The next increase took effect from November 1, 2005 when the government agreed to a return fare of $100.00 on the fast ferries, and to a $75.00 return fare on the conventional ferry. The ferry service had improved dramatically by then and the travelling public considered the increases reasonable.

The private sector also became involved. In November 1994, the Chin Lee family attempted to offer a fast service with the *Condor*, a small catamaran with a complex engine. The vessel completed the journey between Trinidad and Tobago in just over 2 hours but she was unsuited for the rough seas. Some passengers became ill from the rolling of the vessel and it was not unusual for ambulances to be on standby to take traumatised passengers to the hospitals. The *Condor* was taken out of service in April 1995.

CHAPTER IX

2000 to 2005

At the end of the 20th century, the *Panorama* was the only vessel on the route. Passengers and the business community raised their voices once again. It was time for the traditional Christmas shopping in Trinidad and for businesses to import their stock. Tobago had long turned from being an exporter of agricultural goods to Trinidad to being a major importer of such goods from Trinidad, Grenada and St. Vincent. Goods were piling up on the docks. Vendors, consumers and businessmen in Trinidad and in Tobago were frustrated.

The Port Authority eventually responded by barging cargo from Trinidad while the passenger service limped along.

The government (UNC) was forced to take action.

The *m.v. Beauport*

On November 28, 2000 the motor vessel *Beauport* arrived on charter at a daily rate of US $13,000.

Her maiden voyage was low key. Port and government officials together with the media travelled from Port of Spain to Scarborough on December 6. There was a small reception on board and the vessel returned to Trinidad a few hours later.

The *Beauport* did 18 knots, could carry 220 cars and 800 passengers, and contained more passenger cabins than the *m.f. Panorama*. The cabins, with self-contained bathrooms, were located on deck level.

The port at the Tobago terminal in Port of Spain was too shallow for her draft and at first she would dock at the cruise ship terminal. Buses transported passengers between the terminals. The harbour was eventually dredged.

The *Beauport* and the *m.f. Panorama* ran together until December 2004.

In January, 2005 the *Beauport* was used mainly as a cargo vessel with a reduced passenger load except during the Carnival and Easter period.

Her wet lease terminated on June 30, 2005.

The *m.v. Sonia*

The *Sonia* arrived in Tobago on December 21, 2004 on a wet lease from International Shipping Services for US$24,000 per day.

She first called at Scarborough where there was a welcome ceremony. High-ranking public officials and the media toured the vessel. The D.A.C. opposition in Tobago questioned the vessels call at Scarborough and answered themselves - by saying that the P.N.M. were using the ferry service as an election tool (the T.H.A. elections were to be held in January 2005).

The *Sonia* could not take passengers to Port of Spain because she had to be checked for seaworthiness and obtain her licence to engage in coastal trading before she could go into service. All these activities were to be done in Port of Spain.

The *Sonia* was even more spacious than the *Beauport* and had 77 passenger cabins, including a few designed for the physically challenged – a first on the inter-island ferry.

She carried 840 passengers and 200 cars.

Many passengers were to experience a visit to Tobago for the first time, and many more had never gone to Tobago by ferry. But the photographs of the *Sonia* in the media had aroused their curiosity.

First time passengers came from many parts of Trinidad, e.g., Maloney, Chaguanas, Couva, San Fernando, St. Joseph, Belmont, Diego Martin, Curepe, Princes Town, Arouca, Fyzabad, Woodbrook, Morvant, St. Ann's and Cascade. Tobago passengers arrived in Port of Spain on December 29 at 4:30 a.m. on the *Beauport* and lined up for the *Sonia's* inaugural sailing scheduled for 8:30 that morning.

Government dignitaries, officials, families, businessmen, the media and nationals who had returned from abroad for the Christmas holiday also lined up to experience the *Sonia's* first sailing.

They all were looking forward to reaching to Tobago in a record 4½ hours. They were not disappointed: reports of the voyage were all positive.

Port officials were pleased. They wanted to provide passengers with a "luxurious" vessel fit for the 21st century. Comfortable reclining seats, spacious, clean restaurant facilities and well-designed cabins were some of the features of the *Sonia*. Passengers started to describe the trip between the islands as a cruise. What was missing was tour guides to identify landmarks and places of interest particularly to schoolchildren.

The port set about trying to change the culture on board the ferry service and announced a string of rules for *Sonia* passengers to follow: no sleeping on the floor; no sleeping across seats; no smoking (this is a smoke-free vessel); no eating and drinking in the cabins.

Some passengers refused to conform to the new ferry culture; they brought their sheets and pillows and foam mattresses and slept on the floor - it didn't matter whether it was a daylight or night sailing. There were passengers who went to bed on the bench seats in the restaurants and snored. In the cabins, smokers removed the smoke detectors and puffed their lives away. Port security was stretched.

Meanwhile, the pilferage continued. The *Panorama* had already lost sheets, pillows and mattresses together with light and plumbing fixtures. The port responded by using sheets that were almost threadbare and by not replacing pillows and reading lamps. Sometimes they even closed off cabins.

The *Sonia* (like the Beauport) was not spared. There were those who helped themselves to blankets, drapes, sheets and light and plumbing fixtures. (The mattresses were too firm to be folded and taken away).

The light fixtures were no doubt dumped in disgust because they could not be attached to domestic fittings - if only the light-fingered had spoken to their colleagues who had cannibalised the *Panorama.*

The port demanded that cabin passengers provide photo identification (the number was duly noted) and a $20.00 refundable deposit before they were given the keys to their assigned cabins. The passengers who returned their keys got back their deposit.

However, cabins were not checked in the presence of passengers, so there was no accountability although the port had passengers' identification details.

In the end, the already heavily subsidised *Sonia* cost taxpayers much more than the charter rate because the port had to replace all stolen items as fast as they were stolen.

On Sunday, January 23, 2006, the *Sonia* sailed out of the Scarborough harbour at the end of her wet lease. The majority of passengers were sad to see her go.

High Speed Ferry Service

The travelling public wanted more on the ferry service, however. As usual, they complained. Luxurious comfort was fine but they wanted to get to their destinations in less time. The increased pace of life demanded faster sea connections between the islands.

In 2002, quite by accident, a group of Assemblymen in the THA was introduced to the prevalence of fast-moving ferries around the world. They were excited by the thought of a 2-hour trip between the islands.

Enthusiasm wavered at times because there were misgivings about the ability of the vessels to cross the Bocas and the open waters of the Atlantic Ocean. The experience with the *Condor* was ever-present. The THA decided to send a 5-member team to the Canary Islands, where the waters between the islands were reputed to be treacherous and where fast ferries were used to connect the islands.

The team returned to Tobago with glowing reports about the fast turnaround time and the smooth sailing of the catamarans over rough waters.

It was now time to convince the central government which would be bearing the cost of the vessels. This took some effort and the government finally decided to charter a fast ferry on a trial run.

Enter the *Cat*

In January 2005 the government signed an agreement with Bay Ferries Limited of Canada for an initial four-month wetlease of a fast ferry, the *Cat*, which could carry 267 cars and 850 passengers and had a speed of 42 knots. The lease ran from January 10 to May 12 at a cost of US $25,000 per day.

The test run between the islands originated in Port of Spain on January 9. It was a *grande z'affaire*. The port management provided on-board entertainment, food and drink for their specially invited guests, among them being Government Ministers, Mayors, Permanent Secretaries, other public officers, Port Authority staff members and the media.

Some of the invited guests invited their own guests, families and friends.

They all began to congregate in the departure lounge from as early as 5.30 a.m. (the vessel was to sail at 8.30 a.m.). Breakfast was served soon after the vessel left Port of Spain on that sunny Sunday morning. Everyone was in high spirits until the vessel entered the Bocas. It became clear that many of the guests, including those in the media, were crossing the territorial waters for the first time.

The seasoned travellers at first watched bemused as the ferry rookies regurgitated breakfast and drink. Throughout the vessel, their moans and groans replaced the sound of music; the stewards were kept busy rapidly replacing vomit bags and offering tablets for sea sickness.

The Master of the vessel, meanwhile, headed to Scarborough at full speed. The *Cat* arrived in Scarborough in a record two hours.

Tobagonians looked on in awe as passenger after passenger stumbled off the vessel and headed for the pharmacy located obliquely opposite the port. The lines were long and the moaning continued in the pharmacy with some passengers declaring their intention to take the plane back to Trinidad. The pharmacy must have had its best day ever for the sale of Gravol.

Media reports of the test run suggested that the ride on the *Cat* was not an enjoyable one, but the run was successful, and the seasoned travelling public was not swayed by reports that were written by newbies.

When the *Cat* went into service she docked in Tobago overnight and left for Port of Spain the next day at 7 a.m. The return trip arrived in Tobago at 6.30 p.m., and each one-way trip lasted 3 hours.[106] The *Cat* became the vessel of choice with the travelling public. It was fast and comfortable with stabilisers that greatly minimized any roll of the vessel.

The recommendation of the 1928 Murphy Sea Communication Committee for a daylight service which "should provide 'a business-man's trip', or "…'quick weekend trip' between the islands", was about to be implemented, nearly 80 years later. The *Cat* made her first weekend return trip[107] on Saturday, January 16 and Sunday, January 17, 2005.

During the lease period, the *Cat* carried 145,000 passengers and 22,000 cars.

The *Cat* leaves and the *Lynx* arrives

The *Cat* left[108] and another high-speed ferry, the *Lynx*, arrived. The *Lynx* was a smaller but faster vessel.

---

[106] The port authorities were concerned about the environmental impact of the backwash and asked the Master to cut his speed.

[107] The quick weekend trip was possible only for those travelling out of Tobago.

[108] From mid-May to mid-October the *Cat* ferries passengers and cars between Maine and Nova Scotia.

The government had wetleased the *Lynx* from the same company, Bay Ferries Limited of Canada, from May 20, 2005. The cost of the lease was US$22,000 per day. The vessel's carrying capacity was 720 passengers and 200 cars.

The weekend schedule was maintained by the *Lynx* but the departure time from Tobago was shifted from 7 a.m. to 6.30 a.m. to accommodate working passengers.

A negative aspect of the fast ferries might be the configuration of seats - they are far apart. There is no more spontaneous conversation between and among strangers - one of the attractions of the conventional ferries. In any case many of the passengers seemed to prefer gazing at the television screens.

The introduction of double sailings

Carnival, Easter, the July-August holidays and Christmas are traditionally the times when local tourism is at its highest and they are the times when the Government Shipping Service traditionally shows its lack of capacity. Carnival (February) and Easter (April) 2005 proved to be different.

The GSS scheduled the *Cat* and the *Sonia* for 2 return trips a day (double sailings). The GSS also

called on the *Panorama* and the *Beauport* to satisfy
the demand from the travelling public to get to and
from Tobago.

Traffic on the sea bridge for Carnival and Easter 2005

Period	Cat	Sonia	Panorama	Beauport
Carnival 2005 (Feb. 4 - 13)	13,196 passengers 1640 vehicles	10,200 passengers 1486 vehicles	996 passengers no vehicles	2,904 passengers 447 vehicles
Easter 2005 (Mar. 25 - 29)	9,538 passengers 1368 vehicles	8,076 passengers 1229 vehicles	2106 passengers 248 vehicles	2409 passengers 286 vehicles

PATT figures

The long school vacation (July - August 2005)
and the Tobago Heritage Festival (July 15 - August
1) challenged the capacity of the vessels. The *Sonia*
and *Lynx* made two return trips each day while the
Panorama maintained its single return trip in a day.
The vessels carried their full passenger loads. This
means that in any one day of the peak period almost
4,000 persons landed in Tobago. Yet there were
those who could not obtain tickets.

Who would give up a 15-minute ride by air?

In October 2000 *Air Caribbean*, the dedicated carrier between Trinidad and Tobago, folded. *BWIA* was immediately called upon to fill the breach. Many went to the Piarco and Crown Point Airports in hope of getting a standby call. Those who were unsuccessful simply returned home. The ferry service was certainly not an option: the trip took an eternity; the boats were too old; you had to spend too long in line. The list of negative comments was justified.

In 2005, the turnaround in boat capacity, speed and reliability created a multitude of ferry *aficionados*. Uncertainty on the air-bridge had opened a new market for the GSS which to its credit immediately responded with double sailings.

However, the ease with which one could now travel between the islands raised matters of security that the port leadership had to confront. The criminal elements in either of the islands now had the opportunity to get quickly from one island to the next; drug trafficking and gun toting could be practised with impunity. While Trinidad was grappling with a mounting crime rate, Tobago was concerned about the impact of spillover crime on its tourist industry and the safety of its residents.

Port security therefore demanded first that all travellers over the age of fifteen should present photo identification as a precursor to receiving a boarding pass. The identification card was then checked against the boarding pass before the passenger left the departure gate. This was done to ensure that passengers who were about to go on board were holding valid boarding passes in their names. Next, port security introduced body scans and scanners for all passengers and their luggage. Motor vehicles became subject to random searches. Closed circuit television was to be installed on the vessels.

The public face of sea travel between the islands had changed but port security, despite bravely declared plans, often lapsed.

The *Cat* returns

The *Cat* returned on wet lease on October 26, 2005. After the required survey and the completion of the training sessions for the on-board staff, the vessel went into service from Scarborough on October 31 at 6.30 a.m.

At the same time, the faster but smaller *Lynx* left Port of Spain, making it the first time that it was possible to get from one island to the next and return the same day, each day of the week.

It had taken 77 years for the recommendation of the Murphy Committee to be finally realised.

Customer Service

In its 1980 report the Ryan Commission stated: "The Government Shipping Service is...not autonomous and its employees come from various departments within the Port Authority. There is hardly any specialized or expert knowledge in the handling of passengers or catering to them...As a result, users of the Shipping Service are treated as cargo rather than as guests."

Over the years, customer service has not appeared to rank high on the agenda of ferry operations.

Numerous critical "Letters to the Editor" and articles have appeared in the local press about the ferry service. The majority of the letters have related stories of unsatisfactory staff attitude, the inadequacy of the service, lack of information, the absence of crowd control at peak periods and the perception of the ticketing staff holding back tickets for "family and friends". These complaints have been openly expressed at the ticketing offices and elsewhere.

In April 2003 the PATT introduced the computerised Booking Information and Ticketing System (BITS) to manage the sale of tickets, but the public is still convinced that tickets are being held for "family and friends."[109]

At peak periods port security usually secured their persons rather than face the frequently frustrated and unruly crowds that sought to make bookings. On sail dates, the peak period ritual was enacted: passengers were abusive and disorderly - they broke down doors and converged on the vessels with or without confirmed tickets.

The demands on the ferry service had long before outstripped the physical structures in Port of Spain and in Scarborough. The queues were long and slow-moving; the staff held lunch time to be sacred, so customer service was routinely interrupted when that hour came. All ticketing operations ceased at 11 a.m. In the late 1990s the port management decided that ticket sales would continue during the lunch hour but at times no relief clerk was available to the public.[110]

- continues on page 155

---

[109] Over-bookings continue to plague the organisation, particularly at peak periods.
[110] The working day started at 7 a.m. with a lunch break from 11 a.m.

144

A SLICE OF FERRY HISTORY IN COLOUR

m.v. Tobago before she was painted blue in 1976
Photo: Desmond Basso.

The m.f. Gelting South. There were 2 Geltings: Gelting North and Gelting South. The Gelting South travelled between Trinidad and Tobago

The m.v. Tobago leaves the Chaguaramas dry dock

Photo: Desmond Basso.

The m.f. Panorama raises her ramp as she leaves the Scarborough port at 11:00 p.m. (1999)

Photo: Clarence Clarke.

The Condor seems large and powerful against the Scarborough terminal but she could not contend with the power of the Bocas and the currents of Scarborough (1995)

Photo: Desmond Basso.

The m.v. Beauport in Port of Spain PATI.

Photo: courtesy PATI.

The m.v. Sonia in Port of Spain. The port authority chartered this vessel to provide "travel with dignity" to ferry users

Photo: courtesy PATT.

The Cat in Port of Spain. This vessel introduced ferry users to the Catamaran experience

Photo: courtesy PATT.

The Lynx in Port of Spain. This vessel was smaller but faster than the Cat

Photo: courtesy PATT.

An aerial view of the new Scarborough port

Photo. Clement Williams.

In 2004 the PATT employed a Change Manager who functions as the Chairperson of a Ferry Management Team which introduced a range of different approaches for improved customer service.

Among the changes implemented were:

- employment and training of customer service representatives

- the introduction of a staff roster that offers booking service without lunchtime interruptions

- publication of the sailing schedule in the newspapers

- publication of advertisements and commercials in the media advising customers about the sale of tickets

- preparation of palatable meals in the cafeterias (the SWWTU took up this challenge and operated the cafeteria on the *Sonia*)

- accommodation under tents for those doing business at peak periods

- orderly and port-managed passenger boarding.

In 2005 order prevailed. The port security was visible. The checking-in process was properly coordinated and boarding was orderly for the first time in ferry service peak-period history.

However, the staff members who face public abuse worked, and continue to work, in a very cramped space and under deplorable conditions particularly in Port of Spain. In the office there is little space for the necessary desks and chairs. In Port of Spain ticketing services and the departure lounge share the same space. The clerks who check in passengers with motor vehicles operate in makeshift structures that seem on the verge of collapse. The port management has taken notice, and started construction of a new terminal in 2005. The terminal is expected to be completed in early 2006 but progress on the building is slow.

Tobago's port terminal, on the other hand, was completed in early 1990 but the ticketing and passenger boarding capacity has become inadequate.

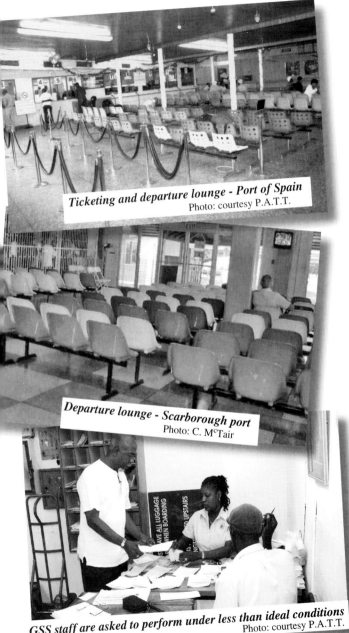

Ticketing and departure lounge - Port of Spain
Photo: courtesy P.A.T.T.

Departure lounge - Scarborough port
Photo: C. McTair

GSS staff are asked to perform under less than ideal conditions
Photo: courtesy P.A.T.T.

Postscript

The government announced in 2004 that the Port Authority would be disbanded and three new companies formed to manage and operate the business of the ports of Port of Spain and Scarborough.[111] The Trinidad and Tobago Inter-island Transport Company will be responsible for the ferry service, its offices in Tobago and Port of Spain, and the port of Scarborough.

The Ryan Commission had recommended the creation of a "separate authority which would accept as its unequivocal responsibility the establishment of an efficiently run sea service to Tobago. The Authority ought to be established in a manner which gives it flexibility and autonomy to carry out *inter alia* the functions of:-

- owning or chartering ships;

- effectively marketing the service of the shipping line;

- acquiring and disposing of all necessary equipment in the operation of the service;

[111] In January 1994 the then Minister of Works had promised a privatised ferry service by June that year. (*Trinidad Guardian*, January 6, 1994, p.1).

- controlling (recruiting and disposing of) all administrative staff, crew and port labour engaged in the operation of the service;

- keeping up-to-date accounting and all necessary statistics which will reflect the operation of service;

- pursuing all those activities which are vital to the effective operation of a shipping service."

On September 29, 2004, the then Port Authority Chairman, Noel Garcia, promised ferry users[112] in Tobago that in the short term the service would deliver an improved passenger service, greater flexibility in sailings, improved turnaround for flatbeds, and increased sailings for cargo.

Port chairmen, their boards and top managers may have reasonable expectations but the final decisions on ferry matters rest with the government.

---

[112] At the meeting were representatives of the Vendors' Association, the Truckers' Association, the Chamber of Commerce, other business interests, the tourism industry, the postal service, hoteliers, Immigration and the Works and Infrastucture Division of the Tobago House of Assembly (THA).

The history of the ferry service shows that successive governments have taken their time to make critical decisions even though the travelling public and businesses are and will be inconvenienced.

What will always remain valid, however, is the description of the ferry service that A.P.T. James gave in 1958[113]:

> "The shipping service between Trinidad and Tobago is as essential to Tobago as the Churchill-Roosevelt Highway, the Eastern Main Road or the Southern Main Road is to Trinidad."

---

[113] *Trinidad Guardian,* January 20, 1958, p. 7.

A FEW OF THE FERRY MASTERS

Cpt. Lorenzo Bodden
Photo: courtesy Shawn Bodden

Cpt. Herman Ashton

Cpt. Theophilus Bess

Cpt. Alfred McMillan

Cpt. Lloyd de Roche

Cpt. Daryll Brizan

Nicole Quashie Chief Mate on the Panorama in 1999. She was promoted to captain in March 2004 making her the 1st female Master on the ferry service

Cpt. Kimraj Gangaram - A former cadet on the Panorama was promoted to Master in March 2004

A FEW OF THE CHIEF ENGINEERS ON THE FERRY SERVICE

Alan Goddard
Photo: courtesy Joe Goddard

William Dottin
Photo: courtesy Desmond Basso

2nd engineer Stanford Stewart (2nd left) enjoys a photo opportunity while 3rd engineer Desmond B(
checks equipment in the Scarlet Ibis engine room. Both Stewart and Basso became chief engineers
Photo: courtesy Desmond Basso

Davidson Hackett

Local Masters and Chief Engineers[114]

Vessels	Masters	Chief Engineers
s.s. Trinidad	Lorenzo Bodden - Rowley [115] Cecil T. Lewis	Alan Goddard - Davis [115] Louis Bento
s.s. Tobago	Cleveland Bodden Orme Clarke Cecil T. Lewis Eustace Urquhart	Alan Goddard Carlton Goddard Cuthbert Alexander Alex Smith
Scarlet Ibis	Lorenzo Bodden Eric Hall Herman Ashton Edgar Johnson	William C. Dottin Cuthbert Alexander Desmond Basso David Robinson Stanford Stewart (acting)

[114] Many of the early Masters lived in Trinidad and Tobago but were originally from other Caribbean islands – Cayman Islands, St. Vincent, Barbados, Grenada.

[115] No one could remember their first names.

Local Masters and Chief Engineers

Vessels	Masters	Chief Engineers
Bird of Paradise	Lorenzo Bodden	Desmond Baldwin
	Bill Ellis	Cuthbert Alexander
	Wilfred Edwards	Hugh Gooding
	Walter Forde	
	Herman Ashton	
	Eustace Urquhart	
	Theophilus Bess	
m.v. Tobago	Eric Hall	Desmond Basso
	Herman Ashton	David Daniel
	Michael Brizan	Davidson Hackett
	Lloyd de Roche	Dorant Jack
	Theophilus Bess	Garth Alleyne
	Alfred Mc Millan	
m.f. Panorama	Herman Ashton	Ewart Brown
	Alfred McMillan	David Daniel
	Nicole Quashie	David Robinson
	Kimraj Gangaram	Davidson Hackett

The journey between Trinidad and Tobago
Map: courtesy PATT.

THE TRADE ROUTE BETWEEN PORT OF SPAIN AND SCARBOROUGH
(excerpts)

From Port of Spain

"Vessel leaves alongside Coastal Steamer Wharf and heads in the direction of the #5 Channel Beacon; when the #5 Channel Beacon comes abeam to port, ring full away on main engines, this is the commencement of the sea passage. From position abeam of #5 Channel Beacon, lay a course to pass half a mile off Nelson Island; when abeam to starboard continue on this course until the First Boca opens to starboard…"

To Scarborough

"When Fort (King) George Light bears North true, steer a course to maintain this bearing until the leading lights at Scarborough come intransit, when leading lights come intransit, alter course for leading lights and steer course to maintain them intransit, when Fort (King) George Light comes abeam to starboard ring standby…

"From position where leading lights come intransit the Master should be on the Bridge and the Courses from thence to alongside should be to Master's orders..."

From Scarborough

"Keep the leading lights intransit astern of the vessel, when Fort (King) George Light comes abeam to port, ring Full Away on the main engine, when Fort (King) George Light bears north true, alter course to south true..."

To Port of Spain

"From position with Fort George Light bearing North true lay a course to pass two miles off North Post...continue on this course until the First Boca opens to port...

"From position where First Boca [116] opens to port to alongside Coastal Steamer Wharf,

---

[116] Inter-island vessels initially passed through the Boca de Monos (1st Bocas) but after several complaints about the Panorama backwash, the route was changed to the Boca de Huevos (2nd Bocas). The wider Boca Grande (3rd Bocas) is the entry and exit for international vessels coming into and leaving Trinidad.

the Master should be on the bridge and the courses should be to Master's orders.

"The Officer of the watch when handing over the watch to another officer should indicate the position of the vessel by Observation or Dead Reckoning (D.R.) on the chart, if he fails to do so, the Master should be consulted to ascertain the vessel's position which in reality of handing over a watch is of paramount importance."

The Trade Route is ruled permanently in ink on maritime maps.

m.f. Panorama
Photo: Clarence Clarke.

From Captain To Cook

The *m.f. Panorama* carries 700 passengers. On board are men and women who "love the sea". Who are these men and women and what do they do?

The Captain/Master is in overall command of the vessel. He gives orders to the Chief Mate, the Chief Engineer and the Chief Steward.

The lines of command are clear. Orders from the captain are then passed on to the crew in the three departments – Stewards, Deck and Engine Room.

The Chief Steward plans the daily menu for the Captain and crew; ensures their meals are served on time; orders stock; oversees the operation of the bar and cafeteria; and is held responsible for untidy cabins.

Not too long ago, the Chief Steward's position was a man's job. Now women have joined the ranks.

The stewards serve the Captain and crew and passengers at the cafeteria and bar. You will also find them at the Information Desk. They are graduates of the Trinidad and Tobago Hospitality Institute or other recognised institution that offers catering courses.

In the Stewards Department, there are five cooks – all men. "Male cooks are part of shipping tradition. Pots are very heavy," says one of the Chief Stewards.

The Stewards (male and female) live on board and get one trip off each week. They work for six days each week, including weekends.

The Stewards Department is the frontline section of the vessel. They do all the interfacing with passengers.

Deckside, the Chief Mate manages his second and third mates and the Boatswain.

The Chief Mate also controls the loading of cargo, flatbeds and vehicles. He carefully and quietly oversees this operation. He has to make sure vehicles and cargo are so placed in the hold that the vessel remains stable, upright and even-keeled.

In addition to these tasks, the Chief Mate is the recognised medical officer. About three years ago (1996), Chief Mate Terrence Percilla delivered a baby girl on board. Mother and child are still doing fine. No! She was not named Panorama; she was not named Terrence. Her first name is Ocean.

Still deckside, the Boatswain is the sailors' foreman. Reporting to the Boatswain are the Able-Bodied Seamen (ABS) and the Ordinary Seamen (OS).

The ABS are certified sailors. They paint, chip rust, splice rope and cable wires, grease the wires on the lifeboats... There is no end to these important tasks. The OS are trainees. They mop and clean and assist the ABS.

The Chief Engineer manages the Engine Room. With him are three officers (a second-class engineer and two third-class engineers), five motormen or oilers and an electrician. The engineers monitor and correct any malfunction of equipment on board. Like the sailors, they perform essential repairs and maintenance.

Nothing is taken for granted on board. Everyone must practise safety measures and be prepared for all emergencies. The Captain and crew have regular fire, lifeboat and other emergency drills since all statutory obligations must be met....

On board the *Panorama* an orchestra is playing. You can't hear the music but the sections know their parts well. The officers are the tenors; the sailors, the double seconds; the stewards, the guitar pans and the engine room is the Engine Room (David Rudder reminds us how vital this section is). The Master and the Chief Engineer blend the sounds that come from deckside and the engine room.

(C. McTair)

Motmot Times, Tobago, Issue 5, Jan/Mar. 1999

CHAPTER X

Legislation

The Customs and Droghers Acts

The Customs Act, Chap. 78.01, PART IX, gives the Customs Department control over all vessels involved in what is called the "Coasting Trade", which is defined as "all trade by sea or air from one part of Trinidad and Tobago to another part and all aircraft and ships while employed therein shall be deemed to be coasting aircraft and coasting ships…"

However, aircraft and ships from places outside Trinidad and Tobago with cargo to be delivered at more than one port are not considered to be coasting vessels although they too are subject to regulations made under the Customs Act.

Vessels attached to the ferry service, barges, boats, and other vessels that move from port to port in the country are, therefore, subject to Customs control.

The Master of the vessel has to maintain a "cargo book" which lists the type and quantity of cargo and the number of passengers, if any, on the vessel. Before the vessel leaves a port, the Master has to report to the Customs, report on his cargo and have his cargo book signed by a Customs officer. As soon as the vessel arrives at the next port the Master must go directly to the Customs Department so they can verify that he arrived only with the contents certified at the outgoing port.

The Master of the *Belize*, for example, had to account for his cargo and passengers on every trip. The Harbour Master would then issue a press release in which he gave all the details contained in the cargo book and the passenger manifest.

The *Port of Spain Gazette* of January 1, 1932 carried the following Government Notice issued by the Harbour Master's Office:

"The *s.s. Belize* returned to P.O.S. yesterday on its 97th trip with the following passengers *(list of names published)*.

"The cargo comprised 311 bags cocoa, 42 bags copra, 8 bunches plantain, 31 pumpkins, 53 packages vegetables, 2 packages corn, 42 head livestock and 5 pot fowls."

Vessels attached to the ferry service are now administratively exempt from presenting a cargo book. The Comptroller of Customs varied the procedure for the ferry service under Section 193 of the Customs Act because it was argued that the ferry service is government-owned and operated and vessels would be tied up for hours if Customs were to enforce the law and check every bit of cargo on board.

Nevertheless, under the Droghers Act the Port Authority (the government's agent) must have a valid "Licence to Navigate Coastwise" for each vessel on the ferry service.

There are a few steps that the owner of a vessel or his representative must take before approaching the Customs Department for a licence to navigate coastwise.

First, he has to pay the necessary taxes. The Cabinet has the power to waive the taxes (this is done for vessels on the ferry service). Second, having paid the taxes, he takes the receipt and other documents to the Maritime Services Division of the Ministry of Works and Transport whose surveyor examines the vessel for seaworthiness and verifies that it is designed to carry passengers, if that is the intention. Vessels on the ferry service are not exempt from this procedure. If the vessel passes inspection, the Maritime Services Division then issues a "Certificate of Seaworthiness."

This is the point at which the Customs Department enters the process. With his tax receipt and "Certificate of Seaworthiness", the owner delivers a return in writing on a special form on which he gives the name of the owner or owners and the name and registered tonnage of the vessel. The Customs Department then inspects the vessel to ensure that details on the form and the vessel's Certificate of Registry correspond with the vessel in port. If satisfied, the Customs Department grants, on payment of specified fees, the Drogher's Licence, sometimes called the "Licence to Navigate Coastwise." The Licence expires on December 31 regardless of when the initial license is granted.

Before the vessel sets out to sea, coastwise, the name must be painted on each quarter of the vessel in lettering that is plain and legible and of a size stipulated by the Act. There is a fine for non-compliance.

The Droghers Act also covers the registration and licensing of sailors who work on vessels engaged in the coasting trade, including those employed in the Government Shipping Service. The Harbour Master (Maritime Services) keeps a book called the Register of Sailors in which the names of all those who are licensed under the Act to operate as sailors, and their licence numbers, are recorded. Sailors' licences all expire on December 31 and are renewable for a small fee.

However, according to Section 12 of the Act, "If any sailor has been convicted of larceny, it shall be lawful for any Harbour Master to make an order cancelling the licence of the sailor, and to withhold the granting of a licence to the sailor so convicted for any term not exceeding two years from the date of conviction."

It is unlawful for an unregistered sailor to work on a coastal vessel and both he and the employer are liable to fines.

Port Authority Ordinance, 39 of 1961
Part IX

(1) The Authority shall operate the Government Shipping Service, in this part referred to as the "service", as the agent of the Government of Trinidad and Tobago, and subject to such regulations as may be made by the Governor in Council in that behalf.

(2) The rates to be paid in respect of passengers and freight in the operation of the service shall be fixed by regulations made by the Governor in Council.

The Authority shall in no circumstances finance or subsidise the service from surpluses accruing from the operation of port services.

The Authority shall keep separate accounts in respect of the service which shall show –

(a) the revenues and costs, and

(b) the surpluses or deficits resulting from the operation of the service.

Any deficit in any year arising out of the operation of the service shall be met by a subvention from the Government that shall amount to the deficit suffered by the operation by the Authority of the service for that year.

A surplus in any year arising out of the operation of the service shall be transferred to a special account to be kept by the Authority and, subject to the discretion of the Governor in Council, shall be used either –

(a) to offset any deficit arising out of the operation of the service in any year or years, or

(b) for such other purpose as the Governor in Council may determine.

Glossary

Bulldog Reef	The entry to the Scarborough Port is extremely difficult to navigate because the area is replete with reefs. The most dangerous is Bulldog Reef which is reputed to be able to slice a ship's hull as easily as a hot knife goes through butter.
Certificate of Registry	The document that contains the registration of a ship's country. The *m.f. Panorama* is a ship of Trinidad and Tobago registry.
invasion barge	a vessel, usually flat-bottomed, that can land on a beach or close to shore so that the armed forces can easily move from the vessel to invade a territory. (A familiar scene in World War II films.)
m.f.	motor ferry

Moses / bum/ surf boats	Small cargo boats that hang on the side of steamers much like life boats are seen today. The boats also carried passengers.
m.v.	motor vessel
Port	"…place whether on the coast or elsewhere, appointed by the President by Notification subject to any conditions or limitations specified in such Notification, to be a port for the purposes of the Customs laws…" Chap. 78.01 – Definitions. In October 1999, the President by Notification (Legal Notices 203 and 204) named Cedros and Charlotteville as ports. These two bays were formally sufferance wharves when the *Belize*, the *Trinidad* and the *Bird of Paradise* called.

Ransomes	A type of fork-lift
Ro/Ro	Roll-on/roll-off. Vehicles and machinery can move directly from the wharf to the hold of the vessel and vice versa.
s.s.	steamship
Sufferance wharf	"…any place other than an approved place for loading and unloading at which the Comptroller may in his discretion, and under such conditions and in such manner as he may direct, either generally, or in any particular case, allow any goods to be loaded or unloaded…" (Customs Laws – Definitions)

Survey Types	
(a) Classification	Since the 18th century Classification Societies assist underwriters in assessing marine risks. The societies require vessels to be constructed and engineered according to set rules. Vessels so constructed are assigned a "class" by the society. Lloyd's of London classifies vessels for the Port Authority.
(b) Continuous	All machinery is divided into surveys which must be undertaken every five years. Tailshaft and oil glands, for example, are examined on dry dock every five years to check their condition and to carry out any repairs that are needed.

Survey Types	
(c) Docking	Underwater portions such as the propeller, rudder and hull are to be surveyed every 2½ years to check their condition and to have repairs effected.
(d) Annual	Every year the general condition of the vessel is examined. The surveyor also searches for any damage that may have an effect on seaworthiness.
(e) Special	Every four years, the vessel is inspected and owners are given a grace period in which to complete repairs.

The Bocas	The correct name is the Dragon's Mouths (Bocas del Dragón). Located at the north of the Gulf of Paria, it is an area of very rough waters. The Serpent's Mouth (Boca del Serpiente) is located at the southern end of the Gulf of Paria. The waters were named by Christopher Columbus who was reported to have been astounded by the ferocity of the waves.
Wet lease (n/v)	Hire of a vessel and its crew for a contracted period.

Index

187